Bob Mooney

2022

What Leaders Are Saying

"Dr. David Stevens and Bert Jones have nailed down, in understandable short principles, how the kind of leadership that really matters influences other people's lives. Two minutes each day, absorbing this clear advice in *Servant Leadership* could be the daily catalyst for success of any organization."
—PETER E. DAWSON, DDS
FOUNDER, THE DAWSON ACADEMY

"Pointed, pithy and powerful. I find Dr. David Stevens' and Bert Jones' writing on point. I move from conviction to affirmation and motivation. I pray often to be the slave of God. These proverbs actualize that prayer."
—DR. JOHN NEIHOF
PRESIDENT, WESLEY BIBLICAL SEMINARY

"With keen insight and wisdom, Dr. David Stevens and Bert Jones have shared nuggets of truth that will inspire and mobilize leaders to become genuine Christ-like servant leaders. If leaders will learn and practice these proverbs, they will discover the joy and multiplied influence of leadership as servanthood."
—DOUG CARTER
SENIOR VICE PRESIDENT, EQUIP

"There is no question we live in a world in desperate need of Godly leadership. In order to truly picture what this looks like, today's influencer need not look further than the principals and practices of Jesus where, as a servant, He led those closest to Him and prepared them to do the same. In this valuable leadership resource, Bert Jones and Dr. David Stevens present time-tested principals in a practical, usable way to help you and your team have the most possible influence for the kingdom. *Servant Leadership* is utilized by our leadership teams at every level, and it is a must have for today's Christian leader.
—NATHAN ALPERT
PRESIDENT, YUGO MINISTRIES

"Being a servant leader is the goal. And this book is the 'how to' manual for reaching that goal. The words of warning, encouragement and instruction are so practical. Built on the foundation of Scripture, these words of wisdom point us toward leadership characteristics that will truly impact those around us. Great resources for leaders who want to make a difference."
—CHAD STUCKEY
PRESIDENT/CREATIVE DIRECTOR, BRAND INNOVATION GROUP

"As business leaders, there is no better way to serve God than by serving man. We all have that opportunity as leaders in our home, businesses and communities. *Servant Leadership* not only will bless and encourage you, like it has me, but it will also give you valuable directions that can be incorporated into your day."

—TROY HENDERSON
EXECUTIVE VICE PRESIDENT, NUTRAMAX LABORATORIES

"*Servant Leadership: Proverbs for Today's Leaders* is a fast-track to success. Dr. David Stevens and Bert Jones have captured the results of their years of leadership experiences and put them into easy-to-read and understand statements that will transform you and the people you serve and lead. It's the behavior of people that influence whether goals and objectives will be achieved, and determine of how much energy it will take to get where you want to go. If you want to ensure success for yourself and for those you serve and lead, integrate a few servant leadership proverbs into your daily discussions and make servant leadership the foundation upon which you and your team are built. Open and frequent discussions about a few proverbs each day will change behavior, align focus and reduce the energy needed to accomplish great things."

—OLIN M. WILAND
ENTREPRENEUR, ADVISOR AND BUSINESS LEADER

"Dr. David Stevens and Bert Jones have scored a second home run in this follow-up volume to their first book, *Leadership Proverbs*. *Servant Leadership: Proverbs for Today's Leaders* is also filled with gems of leadership wisdom, laid out in an easy-browsing format. I love that this book is packed with wisdom, instead of padded with verbiage. The novice leader may mistakenly think that these entries are lightweight because they are concise, but the seasoned leader will read page after page thinking to him or her self, 'Why didn't I have this book earlier in my ministry life? I may not have had to learn so many of these lessons the hard way!' I found myself nodding and reflecting on so many situations where just a line or two from this book would have helped me walk through some of the leadership minefields that we all must traverse. The wise leader will be tempted to devour these pithy thoughts in one sitting. But don't do it! Take the authors' advice and chew slowly, letting the wisdom soak into (and affect) your thinking. I recommend this book highly for all who would lead as servants for Jesus' sake.

—REV. STEVE JONES
PRESIDENT, MISSIONARY CHURCH USA

"I love this new book. Wisdom flows thought the hundreds of uplifting, thought provoking sayings. Let the wisdom of this book help you become the leader God is calling you to be. Every Christian leader should have this book on his or her desk."

—FRANK LOFARO
PRESIDENT, PRISON FELLOWSHIP INTERNATIONAL

"*Servant Leadership: Proverbs for Today's Leaders* is a tremendous resource as it offers trusted wisdom to the realities facing today's leaders. Servant leadership is a paradox for many people and can be difficult to understand and live, yet it always brings about positive major transformation in persons and organizations. The prescription Dr. Stevens provides in the preface for how to use these proverbs delivers a solid guidebook to leaders so that they can transform the world in which we live."

—MARIO R. DICKERSON, MTS
EXECUTIVE DIRECTOR, CATHOLIC MEDICAL ASSOCIATION

"Once again, the power duo of Bert Jones and Dr. David Stevens delivers relevant and timeless leadership proverbs. This powerful collection of servant leadership wisdom is a daily must-read for leaders in business or beyond who seek to follow Jesus' example by placing others above themselves and are leading to help their teams fulfill God's calling for their professional and personal lives. These words will help teams focus on finding significance in each other, and each other's work, that will inevitably lead to greater productivity, attitudes and success."

—ERIC EDWARDS, MD
VICE PRESIDENT OF PRODUCT STRATEGY, KALÉO

"I've had the privilege of working with and closely observing both authors of this book. Their leadership wisdom does not come from theories or textbooks, it has been learned firsthand. I'm so grateful they have taken the time to share it. Like the book of Proverbs from the Bible, if you take the advice given in *Servant Leadership*, you will become wise and prosper!

—RON HOUP

PRESIDENT & CEO, GO INTERNATIONAL

"Much is written on servant leadership, but Dr. David Stevens and Bert Jones have distilled proverbs of wisdom for the leader servant, those who are truly focused on kingdom impact and influencing those around them. There is much that vies for our attention, thought and energy. These bite-sized proverbs are potent to drive our thought and inspiration toward greater influence on those we are called to serve, a much needed daily source of nourishment.

—GREGG CAPIN

PARTNER AND CHAIRMAN, CAPIN CROUSE

This is a great gift book for leaders. It is like a daily dose for 31 months of leadership wisdom medicine. It can cure a lot of leadership ills.

—BRUCE JOHNSON

PRESIDENT, SIM USA

PRESENTED TO

FROM

Servant Leadership

PROVERBS FOR TODAY'S LEADERS

DAVID STEVENS, MD, MA (ETHICS)

BERT JONES

THE CHRISTIAN MEDICAL & DENTAL ASSOCIATIONS WAS
founded in 1931 and currently serves more than 20,000 members;
coordinates a network of Christian healthcare professionals for
personal and professional growth; sponsors student ministries in
medical and dental schools; conducts overseas healthcare projects for
underserved populations; addresses policies on healthcare, medical
ethics and bioethical and human rights issues; distributes educational
and inspirational resources; provides missionary healthcare
professionals with continuing education resources; and conducts
international academic exchange programs.

FOR MORE INFORMATION
Christian Medical & Dental Associations
P.O. Box 7500
Bristol, TN 37621-7500
888-230-2637
www.cmda.org • main@cmda.org

Second Printing – 2021

ISBN 978-0-9897598-7-8
2017933377

Dedication

To Christ, the best role model of servant leadership who ever lived. As He said in Mark 10:44, "and whosoever would be first among you, shall be servant of all" (ASV).

And to my staff at Christian Medical & Dental Associations who demonstrate extraordinary servant leadership daily. A great joy of my life is having the privilege of leading them.

—DAVID STEVENS, MD, MA (ETHICS)

To my wonderful wife Cheryl, who continues to support and encourage my interest in leadership and new challenges in life. Thank you for standing by my side all these years.

To my children, Joshua, Allyson and Aaron, for their leadership, accomplishments and service to others. I am so proud of them.

To the servants and mentors I have worked alongside through the years who have taught me many of the lessons shared in this book.

To the wonderful people, staff and leadership at Woodburn Missionary Church who have allowed me the privilege of serving as their Senior Pastor.

—BERT JONES

Servant leadership is the most effective type of leadership in today's world. But what does it mean to be a servant leader? And how do you do it? You may not know how to practice this type of leadership, but you recognize it when you see it. Though many people are attracted to the concept of being a servant leader in their homes, workplace and community, they don't know how to do it or even where to begin. Old habits and ways of leading are hard to break. In their second collaboration, Dr. David Stevens and Bert Jones use pithy and succinct proverbs to teach you how to become the servant leader you desire to be. And as you apply these principles, you will become the servant leader God designed you to be and influence generations of servant leaders to come.

Table of Contents

Table of Contents (continued)

Introduction

IF YOU LOOK UP THE TERM "SERVANT LEADERSHIP" online, you will find that the phrase was coined by Robert K. Greenleaf in *The Servant as Leader*, an essay he first published in 1970. Yes, he may have coined the term, but the concept itself dates back to Christ, the greatest servant leader who ever lived.

Today, the Greenleaf Institute states, "Servant leadership is a philosophy and set of practices that enriches the lives of individuals, builds better organizations and ultimately creates a more just and caring world." I would wholeheartedly agree, but a better definition of servant leadership is found in Mark 9:35.

In this chapter, Jesus sets down His disciples to conduct a leadership intervention because they were arguing among themselves about who would be the greatest when Christ established His kingdom. Jesus summed up servant leadership in a short phrase, "Anyone who wants to be first must be the very last, and the servant of all" (Mark 9:35).

In Mark 10:42-45, He expands on that by saying,

> *You know that those who are regarded as rulers of the Gentiles lord it over them, and their high officials exercise authority over them. Not so with you. Instead, whoever wants to become great among you must be your servant, and whoever wants to be first must be slave of all. For even the Son of Man did not come to be served, but to serve, and to give his life as a ransom for many.*

If the Son of God was a servant leader, shouldn't we each aspire to be one as well?

Introduction (continued)

Servant leaders are servants first and leaders second. It would be more accurate to call them "leader servants." Their main focus is serving others, not the accumulation of power, prestige or wealth. They want to help those they lead to become all God designed them to be by helping them to reach their full potential. Their goal is not to build an empire but to build the people they influence—their staff, their customers and their communities.

Servant leadership is so effective that it results in the highest form of influence in other people's lives. People may not know how to practice this type of leadership, but they recognize it when they see it. If you ask someone to name a servant leader, Mother Teresa would likely be on the short list. She had no authority, no great title and no riches, and yet, you can't deny she had incredible influence on millions of people around the world.

Servant leaders are not feared; instead, they are loved, respected and praised by their followers. Followers know that such leaders will willingly sacrifice themselves for the good of their followers and the mission of the group. Servant leaders know the true measure of success is building people, so they invest their lives in building others up. They spend time with their staff and influence them by modeling servanthood rather than just talking about it. Their actions match their words and those they lead aspire to be like them.

Servant leaders reproduce themselves in their followers who become servant leaders themselves to influence many more. Thus, this type of leader is contagious, infecting others with the desire to serve. Their influence is exponential and continues far beyond their own lives.

I was "infected" by the example of Dr. Ernie Steury, a humble missionary physician who faithfully modeled servant leadership to me as we served at a small bush hospital he started in rural Kenya in 1959. He was so contagious that I had the overwhelming desire to be just like him after spending only a few weeks following him around as a college student one summer.

After finishing medical school and residency, I joined Ernie as a missionary physician in 1981. His impact on my life was profound as he invested in me for 11 years. He stretched me constantly and gave me ever-increasing responsibilities and authority, essentially providing a "lab" for me to practice what he modeled. He advised, encouraged and challenged me to new heights every day. Four years after I arrived, he put me in charge of the hospital when he traveled back to the United States for a year furlough. As I continue striving to be a servant and build others, I know I'm the leader I am today because of his investment in my life.

Though organizational success is not the primary goal of a servant leader, it is its byproduct because you get the best effort and results out of those you lead. I've experienced this. As the Chief Executive Officer of Christian Medical & Dental Associations, I was surprised when we were selected as the "Best Christian Workplace" in the U.S. by *Christianity Today* and the Christian Leadership Alliance. I was amazed, because we had gone from a struggling small organization that almost imploded due to a huge crisis my first year to an admired major player in the non-profit sector eight years later. I credit that to my senior staff's efforts to be servant leaders.

Though many people are attracted to the concept of being a servant leader in their homes, workplace and community, they don't know how to do it or even where to begin. Old habits and ways of leading are hard to break. That's why Bert Jones and I wrote this book. Using pithy and succinct proverbs, we teach you how to become the servant leader you desire to be. If you are already a servant leader, we will help you further improve "your serve" because you should never be satisfied with where you are on your journey.

So read on and take your medicine. My prescription for you is to take three to four proverbs a day with a glass of resolve and chew well! As you apply these principles, you will become the servant leader God designed you to be and influence generations of servant leaders to come.

—DAVID STEVENS, MD, MA (ETHICS)

Chapter 1

DON'T BE A SERVANT LEADER BUT A leader servant. Be a servant first and a leader second.

1:1 _____

WHAT SHOULD YOU DO WHEN THINGS ARE askew? Review and redeploy the first principles of leadership to right the ship.

1:2 _____

A DEFIANT TEAM MEMBER DISOBEYS, disrupts and disregards the team's purpose and progress. Like a cancer, they must be excised to save the organism.

1:3 _____

A WISE LEADER KNOWS THE DIFFERENCE between a calculated risk and a crazy risk. One can bring triumph and the other tragedy.

1:4 _____

Chapter 1

1:5   EVEN LEADERS WHO ARE LEAVING A GREAT and lasting impression can still battle seasons of serious depression. Get help!

1:6   IN THE LEADERSHIP RACE, STAY THE COURSE no matter the obstacles or criticism. Persevere to prosper.

1:7   LEADERS CAN BLOOM OR BE DOOMED SIMPLY by how their time is consumed. Expend your time on purpose.

1:8   COLLABORATE AND COOPERATE. MANY MINDS multiply wisdom and success (Ecclesiastes 4:9).

BEING ON TRACK DOES NOT GUARANTEE   1:9
everyone will be on board. People will often fight
against the right idea. Use your influence to get them
involved.

EVERY OPPORTUNITY HAS ITS OWN   1:10
opposition. Expect it and, when necessary, overcome
it (1 Corinthians 16:9).

LEADERS CANNOT AFFORD TO HALT PROGRESS   1:11
because they get their feelings hurt. Forgive, forget
and move forward.

YOU MUST BE TOUGH ENOUGH TO LEAD   1:12
through the rough, prickly stuff. Thin-skinned leaders
will perish from a thousand small cuts.

Chapter 1

1:13   REGULARLY REVIEW YOUR TEAM'S ADHERENCE to your corporate values while passionately pursuing your mission.

1:14   IT IS CRITICAL FOR LEADERS TO BE BOTH practical and analytical in their decision-making process. Sometimes that means adding a constructive critic to the decision-making team.

1:15   A LEADER SHOULD BE FANATICAL ABOUT taking a regular sabbatical. Time out is better than burn out (Luke 5:16). A regular day off helps a leader go on.

1:16   SERVANT LEADERSHIP IS MARKED BY THOSE they served growing to become wiser, more autonomous and more likely to become servants themselves.

A GOOD LEADER WILL EXERCISE NEUTRALITY rather than partiality with personnel. Be objective with your evaluations and decisions. Leaders who believe they are bigger than the cause commit a leadership faux pas.

1:17

RATHER THAN LEAP TO CONCLUSIONS, GOOD leaders reach conclusions and then carry them out with conviction.

1:18

PIGHEADED LEADERS ARE SO STUPIDLY stubborn that they stymie their team's success.

1:19

LEADERS NEED TO EARN THEIR TURN TO BE heard. Take time to listen and learn before you speak up.

1:20

Chapter 1

1:21   ANYTIME THERE IS MAJOR DIVISION
surrounding a decision, slow down and reevaluate.

1:22   WHEN LEADERS MASTER THE LITTLE, THEY
will soon have the opportunity to do a lot (Luke 19:17).

1:23   IF IT DOESN'T FEEL RIGHT, IT MOST LIKELY
isn't. Trust your intuition.

1:24   IF YOU ARE DETERMINED ENOUGH, YOU CAN
accomplish almost anything.

IT CAN TAKE YEARS TO ESTABLISH TRUST, BUT
it only takes moments to abolish it. Work hard to
develop trust and then protect it at all cost.

1:25

CONFIDENCE IS NOT A COINCIDENCE. IT IS
established through a consistent character and
successfully exercising your abilities.

1:26

PREPARATION PROMPTS PRODUCTION. THE
more you prepare, the more you will produce.

1:27

SERVANT LEADERSHIP CAN WORK IN ALL
types of situations: in for-profits, in not-for-profits,
in churches, in educational institutions, in healthcare
and in families.

1:28

Chapter 1

1:29   DON'T WAIT ON THOSE WHO ARE LATE TO begin a meeting. Start on time. Don't reward the wayward.

1:30   CHALLENGES ARE OPPORTUNITIES TO demonstrate your capabilities. Don't run from them. Latch on to them.

Chapter 2

CONFRONTING SOMEONE OR SOMETHING is never comfortable. Do it anyway. Problems worsen when they are ignored.

2:1

CONSCIENTIOUS LEADERS ARE NEVER oblivious to their obligations. Don't shirk your leadership duties.

2:2

A LEADER DOES NOT HAVE TO BE ABRASIVE or abrupt to solve a problem. A kind word full of truth is extremely effective.

2:3

TRUE LEADERS ARE NOT AFRAID TO SPEAK with authority about what they believe to be the absolute truth (Luke 4:32). Courageous leaders have strong convictions.

2:4

Chapter 2

2:5   As a servant leader, you may feel deflated at times, but don't let that cause you to be defeated.

2:6   There is a huge difference between interest and investment. One is curiosity. The other is commitment.

2:7   Visionary leaders let their aspirations become inspiration for the next generation's leaders.

2:8   Good advice is ineffective unless the intended recipient is receptive.

FAILURE TO PRODUCE REAL RESULTS WILL,   2:9
over time, significantly reduce a leader's followers.

SEEMINGLY INSIGNIFICANT DECISIONS,   2:10
wrongly made, can have significant repercussions.

DISAPPOINTMENT CAN BE A DIVINE   2:11
appointment if it enhances your leadership.

DECISION FATIGUE CAN DISABLE YOUR   2:12
leadership. Differentiate between what you must do
and what you should delegate.

Chapter 2

2:13   ADDRESS YOUR STRESS BEFORE IT CAUSES YOU to regress.

2:14   TRACK YOUR ACCOMPLISHMENTS. IT WILL encourage you and inspire your followers.

2:15   GOOD ORGANIZATION DOES NOT GUARANTEE the absence of frustration. Leadership has a price tag attached.

2:16   HARDWORKING EMPLOYEES ARE WORTH THEIR weight in gold. Reward them! It is easier to retain good employees than attain new ones.

PROBLEMS, LIKE FIRES, ARE EASIER TO 2:17
extinguish when they're small.

RESPECT IS LIKE GASOLINE. IT CAN FUEL 2:18
your leadership or explode in a millisecond with an
inflammatory response. Handle with extreme care.

SERVANT LEADERSHIP IS NOT A QUICK FIX. ITS 2:19
effect takes time to take over every fiber of your
organization to bring long-lasting transformation.

GUARD YOUR CHARACTER. MOMENTARILY 2:20
dropping your guard can be monumentally
devastating.

Chapter 2

2:21 CRISIS CRIES FOR LEADERSHIP. STEP UP!
Like making a diamond, the pressure will mold you,
strengthen you and make you attractive.

2:22 INPUT IMPACTS OUTPUT. GARBAGE IN.
Garbage out. Be intentional about what you put into
your brain (Galatians 6:7).

2:23 TURNOVER IS INEVITABLE IN THE PROCESS OF
a turn around. Sometimes you have to let go in order
to move in the right direction.

2:24 THE TURNAROUND IS PROPORTIONAL TO THE
size of the problem. You can't turn a jetliner on a
dime. It takes time.

To AVOID EMBARRASSMENT, POSTPONE AN   2:25
event until someone is assigned to plan the event.

INTUITION IS INSIGHT WITHOUT   2:26
information. It's knowing what to do without
knowing why. If you've got it, use it.

INERTIA IS COSTLY TO OVERCOME. DON'T   2:27
forfeit momentum. If you've got it, accelerate!

A LEADER HAS THE PRIVILEGE AND THE   2:28
pressure to produce a creative, compelling and
convicting vision.

2:29 SUCCESS FOSTERS SUCCESS. START WITH what is simple and then tackle what is complicated.

2:30 BACK OFF AND BACK UP TO GET FEEDBACK IN the midst of a setback. It will make a comeback more certain.

2:31 THE MORE EXTREME YOUR DREAM, THE MORE you need a dream team.

2:32 SERVANT LEADERSHIP IS THE STRONG foundation upon which to rest all your other organizational initiatives like quality assurance, continual improvement and system efficiency.

Chapter 3

CONSTRAIN HOW MUCH YOU COMPLAIN.
You won't shine if you whine; you'll just make everyone else wilt.

3:1

TAKE CHARGE OF THE CHANGES YOU NEED TO make. You can either complain about problems or conquer them—the choice is up to you.

3:2

IT'S RIDICULOUS TO SUPPORT A POLICY YOU can't regulate. If you can't enforce it, don't endorse it.

3:3

SERVANT LEADERSHIP IS LESS ABOUT BIG visionary speeches and more about small intimate discussions. It is digging down into the details affecting your team's performance and morale.

3:4

Chapter 3

3:5   IN PURSUIT OF AN INFIELD HOME RUN, TAG
all of your bases or you will be OUT. Covering all
your bases is one of the basics of leadership.

3:6   EFFECTIVE LEADERS DON'T LEAVE CHANGE UP
to chance. They model it, mold it, motivate it and
manage it constantly.

3:7   SERVANT LEADERS: SERVE LONG! SERVE WELL!
Serve consistently!

3:8   YOUR LEADERSHIP SHOULD ELIMINATE WHAT
you won't tolerate within your team.

IT'S OFTEN THE SECOND EFFORT THAT HAS
the greatest effect. Don't give up too soon.
Determination is what gets you to where you want to
go.

3:9

LEADERS SHOULD NEVER REACT BEFORE THEY
have taken the time to reflect.

3:10

IF A LEADER ACTS DEFEATED, THE MORALE ON
the team will be depleted, but if you have courage,
people will be encouraged.

3:11

YOU CAN'T MOTIVATE WHEN YOU
manipulate. Inspire, empower and lead the charge.

3:12

Chapter 3

3:13   NO LEADERSHIP BUBBLE CAN PROTECT YOU from times of trouble. Step up and deal with difficult days.

3:14   IF THERE WERE NO PROBLEMS, NO ONE WOULD need leaders. Prepare and plan for problems so you won't panic when they arrive.

3:15   EMERGING FROM TROUBLED TIMES TAKES patience, prudence, persistence and divine providence.

3:16   IF A PERSON WON'T SUBMIT, THAT PERSON IS not a good fit for leadership. Don't waste your time mentoring them.

CULTIVATE EVEN THE DIFFICULT PEOPLE IN
your world. Some can still be a great help on your
leadership journey.

3:17 _____

⁂

NEVER LET THE FACT THAT YOU CANNOT DO
everything keep you from doing something. Do what
you can with what you have.

3:18 _____

⁂

DON'T LET ONE PERSON DOMINATE OR
complicate the direction or decisions of your
organization.

3:19 _____

⁂

A WISE LEADER USES CREATIVE IMAGES TO
stir imagination and ingenuity.

3:20 _____

Chapter 3

3:21   CONVINCING LEADERS REINFORCE THEIR course with compelling content and conviction.

3:22   YOUR TEAM MAY REBEL IF THEY ARE coerced. Inspire to stay out of that mire.

3:23   ALL THINGS ARE POSSIBLE TO THOSE WHO believe. Convictions break through most restrictions.

3:24   MAKE YOUR LIFE COUNT BY CONCENTRATING on things that are eternal. Care most about what really matters.

CHEAPER IS OFTEN MORE COSTLY. THE BEST buy may not be the best bargain in the long run.

3:25

MAKE SURE THE VIEW YOU HAVE OF YOURSELF is true (Romans 12:3).

3:26

A LEADER MUST REMEMBER TO COMMUNICATE what they contemplate. Followers won't act unless you articulate what's on your mind.

3:27

REPRODUCTION IS MORE IMPORTANT THAN production. Discipline yourself to disciple future leaders.

3:28

Chapter 3

3:29   ENVY IS A TERRIBLE ENEMY OF LEADERSHIP.
It will devour you from the inside out (James 3:16).

3:30   PRESSURE TEACHES LEADERS HOW TO PRESS
on and press through. But be careful, if you take on
too much pressure, you will pop (2 Corinthians 4:8;
Philippians 3:12,14).

3:31   LEADERS MUST LEARN TO PLACE FREE SPACE
into their day in case unexpected interruptions come
their way.

3:32   SERVANT LEADERS DON'T DEMAND TO BE
noticed.

Chapter 4

ANTICIPATE A POSSIBLE SETBACK IF YOU are not receiving honest feedback from your constituents, colleagues and critics. Feedback marks the track to excellence.

4:1 _____

A BIG TASK IS SOON DONE WHEN YOU TACKLE it a little bit every day.

4:2 _____

NEVER ASSUME A DELEGATED TASK IS DONE. Check on it before checking it off your list.

4:3 _____

WHEN YOU DO NOT APPRECIATE YOUR STAFF'S accomplishments, their loyalty and longevity disintegrate.

4:4 _____

Chapter 4

4:5   IT'S NOT UNCOMMON TO HAVE AN appointment with disappointment. People and circumstances can dishearten a leader.

4:6   BEING UNDEFEATED IS OVERRATED. A DECENT defeat can help you compete at a higher level of competency and consistency.

4:7   ATTITUDE ENHANCES A LEADER'S ADVANCE or hinders the cause. Be positive.

4:8   FIND A REASON TO LAUGH; IT GREASES THE frictions of life.

DELEGATE TO RELEGATE FALLING BEHIND.   4:9
Empower others to help you succeed.

SELF-DISCIPLINE REDUCES YOUR LEVEL OF   4:10
regret down the road.

PROCRASTINATION LEADS TO   4:11
consternation. Act on what needs to be done today.

ALWAYS PRODUCE WHAT YOU PROMISE.   4:12

FOLLOW THROUGH ON WHAT YOU THREATEN   4:13
to do; your integrity is at stake.

Chapter 4

4:14   KEEP YOUR LISTENING PRIORITIES IN ORDER:

- God,

- Those in authority over you,

- Those who surround you,

- Those who follow you, and

- Those who oppose you.

You will lose order otherwise.

4:15   SERVANT LEADERSHIP EXPANDS ENGAGEMENT, boosts trust and deepens relationships with your team and those they serve.

4:16   IF CROSSED, THERE ARE SOME LINES OF NO return. Know yours and define them clearly to others.

A NATURAL BORN LEADER WILL CAUSE ALARM   4:17
if they pursue harm. Leadership ability can be used
for good or bad.

SERVANT LEADERS ARE MORE PRODUCTIVE   4:18
because those they influence desire to be more
productive.

DON'T LET SUCCESS STALL YOUR VISION.   4:19
Never be content with the status quo.

LEADERS CAN NEVER AFFORD TO ALLOW   4:20
their dreams to lose steam. Keep fueling it forward.

Chapter 4

4:21   IN THE END, YOU CAN WIN AND GET WHAT YOU want, but lose what you need (Matthew 16:21).

<hr>

4:22   THERE IS ALWAYS HOPE AT THE END OF THE rope. Hold on!

<hr>

4:23   WHEN YOU LOSE, CHOOSE TO USE IT AS AN educational opportunity.

<hr>

4:24   TEMPER YOUR TEMPER. HEADS ROLL WHEN you lose control, yours included. As the Bible says, "Be angry and do not sin" (Ephesians 4:26, ESV).

IT'S WHAT YOU DON'T KNOW THAT CAN DEAL
you the greatest blow. Relentlessly educate yourself.

4:25

A SERVANT LEADER CONDUCTS THE
orchestra. They let everyone play their instruments
well as they coordinate all the sections to make great
harmony.

4:26

KEEP YOUR SANITY BY MINDING YOUR OWN
business. That's enough to keep you busy (1
Thessalonians 4:11).

4:27

AS A FOUNDATIONAL RULE, ALWAYS
formulate your opinions on facts, not your feelings.

4:28

Chapter 4

4:29   DON'T GIVE ADVICE TO OTHERS THAT YOU would not accept or act on if it were given to you. That's called hypocrisy.

4:30   WHEN THINGS GO WRONG, LEADERS DON'T get furious, they get curious as to why and then search for a solution.

Chapter 5

GIVING FOLLOWERS THE AUTHORITY TO do what they do well is one of the marks of a servant leader.

YOUR HOSPITALITY CAN SERVE AS A HOSPITAL of hope for those who are hurting. Be kind to those you come in contact with each day.

IT'S DIFFICULT TO PROCEED AND MAKE progress on a particular project if you don't know its purpose from the start. Take some time to understand before you undertake.

AS A LEADER, YOUR LEGACY IS FORTUNATELY not gaged by your fortune. It's not the money you leave behind but the lives you influence that really count.

5:1 _____

5:2 _____

5:3 _____

5:4 _____

Chapter 5

5:5   REFINE YOUR CHARACTER. IT IS YOUR FIRM foundation. Without it, everything else crumbles.

5:6   EVERYONE IS IMPORTANT, BUT NO ONE IS indispensable, including you.

5:7   DETERMINE TO ENJOY YOUR JOB INSTEAD OF enduring your job. It will make your days go much faster.

5:8   TAKING OWNERSHIP IS A LEADER'S responsibility.

STAND UP AND PROTECT YOUR TEAM. YOU
hold on to people by hanging with them.

5:9 _____

SINCE YOU CAN'T ALWAYS REVERSE YOUR
actions, take a moment to rehearse your actions
before you take center stage. Then you won't flop!

5:10 _____

SIMPLE PERSISTENCE CAN GET YOU THROUGH
some serious resistance.

5:11 _____

LIFE IS A PERFORMANCE, NOT A PRACTICE
session. Give it your very best every time, every day.

5:12 _____

Chapter 5

5:13   DETERMINE WHERE YOU WANT TO GO AND
back up. Determine the first step and take it. Then
take the next step and the next step, until you reach
your destination.

5:14   IF YOU WANT TO MAKE A GREAT CONNECTION
during a conversation, be inquisitive and take a
genuine interest in each response. You can make a
great impression simply through listening.

5:15   THERE ARE TIMES WHEN IT IS NOT RIGHT TO
fight. Just let it go.

5:16   BE CAREFUL NOT TO TAKE SIDES BEFORE YOU
hear the entire story. You look foolish when jumping
to conclusions before knowing all the facts.

ALWAYS SEEK VERTICAL ADVICE BEFORE
reaching a final verdict. Seek God's wisdom before
you act (1 Samuel 23:2).

5:17

WELL-HANDLED ADVERSITY IS A GREAT
advertisement of your leadership.

5:18

A SERVANT LEADER SHARES EQUALLY IN THE
benefits given to the team and bears more than their
share of the burdens.

5:19

GOD WILL TAKE YOU THROUGH DIFFERENT
leadership seasons. There is a reason for the season
you're in right now.

5:20

Chapter 5

5:21   PEOPLE WHO FOCUS ON REVEALING OTHER'S shortcomings are simply trying to cover their own insecurities and insufficiencies.

5:22   DON'T TRY TO DESTROY THE REPUTATION OF another leader to gain power or position. That will boomerang and destroy you.

5:23   LEADERS WILL BE JUDGED ULTIMATELY BY their reputation (are they admired?), by their results (what did they accomplish?) and by their recruits (who are their followers?).

5:24   REFRAIN FROM THE TEMPTATION TO complain. A leader's actions speak louder than words.

APPRAISE YOUR APPRECIATION OF YOUR 5:25
people. Are you communicating in effective ways?
If not, revamp. Intangibles, not money, motivate
extraordinary effort.

IT'S INCREDIBLE WHAT LEADERS CAN 5:26
accomplish when they don't care about accruing the
credit.

MAKE UP YOUR MIND TO KEEP AN OPEN MIND. 5:27
A closed mind closes the doors to future
opportunities.

WHEN PEOPLE TURN THEIR BACKS ON YOU, 5:28
turn the other cheek (Matthew 5:39).

Chapter 5

5:29　SERVANT LEADERS USE THEIR POWER
legitimately and always for the good of the people
they serve.

5:30　YOU'RE READY TO LEAD WHEN YOU REALIZE
you can't, but God through you can (Luke 1:37).

Chapter 6

A LEADER MUST HAVE THE CAPACITY FOR tenacity.

6:1 _____

IF YOU ARE TENTATIVE IN YOUR DECISION-making, you will be ineffective in your leadership.

6:2 _____

A STRATEGIC PLAN SHOULD NEVER BE SET IN stone. It must be adjusted, amended and added to as necessary. Make it dynamic.

6:3 _____

"LIFE'S NOT FAIR!" GET OVER IT AND YOU will get ahead.

6:4 _____

Chapter 6

6:5   THE SERVANT LEADER IS A TEACHER OF HIS team and a learner from his team. This builds mutual respect, honest communication and trust.

6:6   LEADERS WHO ARE BUILDING FOR THE future are intentional investors in the next generation of leaders.

6:7   TO FIND OPPORTUNITIES FOR IMPROVEMENT, solicit the insights of other individuals.

6:8   YOU CAN'T STEER A PARKED CAR. MOVE TO maneuver and gain momentum.

BETWEEN A ROCK AND A HARD PLACE? 6:9
Pray for wisdom and for God to intervene.

THE QUALITY OF YOUR PRESENTATION 6:10
greatly influences the level of the listeners'
participation.

A RESPONSIBLE LEADER HAS A QUICK 6:11
response time to problems and predicaments. Don't
delay by putting it off for another day.

ESTABLISH AND MAINTAIN MOMENTUM TO 6:12
crush inertia.

Chapter 6

6:13   WHEN YOU START SOMETHING, GIVE IT EVERY chance for success. Don't launch without a good strategy.

6:14   NOT EVERYONE WHO DESIRES A POSITION OF leadership should lead. If you are not wired to lead, it will be a miserable experience for everyone.

6:15   YOUR LEADERSHIP STRUCTURE SHOULD NOT be so rigid that you restrain your team's success. Build in some flexibility.

6:16   COLLECT AS MUCH INFORMATION AS necessary to make the correct decision.

PAY ATTENTION TO DETAILS TO ACHIEVE YOUR
dreams. Little things add up to a big thing when done
right.

6:17

TO ATTAIN SOMETHING SIGNIFICANT, YOU
have to be willing to risk something substantial.

6:18

DON'T OVERLOOK, OVERREACT OR
overwhelm when you overhaul your organization.

6:19

THE BEST WAY TO PRESERVE YOUR TEAM IS TO
take action when an individual is burning out. Make
them take a deserved break.

6:20

Chapter 6

6:21 DON'T BELIEVE EVERYTHING YOU READ unless it comes from the Bible.

6:22 ALWAYS ACKNOWLEDGE, CONGRATULATE AND celebrate the accomplishments of people within your world. Servant leaders compliment their competitors.

6:23 REFUSE TO MAKE AN EXCUSE, BUT DON'T hesitate to produce an explanation.

6:24 PURSUE TRUTH AND WISDOM. THEY ARE THE greatest wealth.

SERVANT LEADERS DON'T MAKE EXCUSES.   6:25
They admit their errors, apologize and, if needed, ask
for forgiveness.

WHEN IT COMES TO CHANGE, THERE ARE ONLY   6:26
two types: beneficial and superficial. One impacts
substance, the other only skims the surface.

GIVE YOURSELF A BREAK WHEN YOU MAKE A   6:27
mistake. Educate yourself on what went wrong and
then move along.

THE REAL VALUE OF AN OPPORTUNITY IS   6:28
often more about what you can learn from it than
what you can earn from it.

Chapter 6

6:29   DON'T PRETEND TO COMPREHEND WHEN YOU
don't. Ask for clarification when you don't
understand.

6:30   FIND TIME EVERY DAY TO UNWIND YOUR
mind. Don't elude moments of solitude.

6:31   IT'S ENORMOUSLY EFFECTIVE TO GATHER
another perspective from someone who will be
honest.

Chapter 7

I F YOU RECONSIDER WHAT YOU HAVE refused up until now, your open-mindedness may reveal a new opportunity.

7:1

WHEN IT BECOMES APPARENT TO THE PEOPLE you lead that you are not being transparent, you're in trouble.

7:2

SERVANT LEADERS TRUST, INSPIRE AND empower each team member.

7:3

KEEP A LEADERSHIP JOURNAL OF THE lessons you have learned along your journey. If you take some good notes, you'll have some great quotes to share.

7:4

Chapter 7

7:5   CAST YOUR VISION IN EVERY CONVERSATION;
someone may take the bait and want to get on board.

7:6   GIVE YOUR TEAM THE PRESENT OF YOUR
presence as often as you can. It's a gift that is a real lift
to their morale.

7:7   DEAL WITH PROBLEMS PROMPTLY. DELAY
will not help them go away.

7:8   PURSUE YOUR MISSION WITH PERSISTENCE
even when you encounter great resistance.

KEEP YOUR COMMITMENTS EVEN WHEN IT IS 7:9
no longer convenient. Don't bail on your word
because something better came along.

SERVANT LEADERS FOCUS ON DEVELOPING 7:10
synergistic relationships with the team instead of
setting up tight systems of control.

DON'T BE TENTATIVE WHEN YOU ARE TRYING 7:11
to get someone's attention.

DON'T BE DISCOURAGED OR DISMAYED WHEN 7:12
someone on your team isn't enthused about your
plan. Winsomely win them over.

Chapter 7

7:13   CLEARLY ARTICULATE THE VALUES YOU AND your team must demonstrate as they pursue your organizational mission.

7:14   POOR LEADERS ARE DANGEROUS TO THE organization and abusive to their staff. They can't inspire so they conspire to manipulate and coerce to get their way.

7:15   DON'T DELUDE YOURSELF. WHAT YOU BELIEVE will determine how you behave. Regularly give yourself doses of reality.

7:16   DON'T GET STUCK IN A RUT. A LEADER HAS TO change things up from time to time to keep it fresh.

YOU WILL DEBILITATE A MEETING IF YOU   7:17
don't facilitate a meeting; you will waste everyone's
time.

THERE WILL BE FEWER PROBLEMS IF YOUR   7:18
personnel know the personality profile of each team
member. Being "other-aware" promotes progress.

DON'T GET A BIG HEAD WHEN YOU GET   7:19
ahead. Pride goes before a fall (Proverbs 16:18).

MANNERS MATTER IN LEADERSHIP. IF YOU   7:20
lack them, it will shatter your chances for success.

Chapter 7

7:21 A LEADER'S MANTRA SHOULD BE "DUTY first," not "duty free."

7:22 RELAX BEFORE YOU HIT YOUR MAX. STRESS IS the consequence of no recess.

7:23 BE CORDIAL. IT CUTS DOWN ON DISCORD around the office.

7:24 BEFORE YOU CAN PREVAIL, YOU HAVE TO SELL what your mission entails.

7:25 WHEN YOU ARE LEADING A MEETING, NEVER prolong what you can move along.

PAUSE FOR A MOMENT AND SEE IF YOU'RE
upset with or without cause.

7:26

IF YOU FIRST CONNECT BEFORE YOU CORRECT,
you will have a better effect.

7:27

STREAMLINE YOUR LEADERSHIP STRUCTURE
until it is efficient and effective. It's harder to
accomplish a task when the structure is too
complicated. Keep the structure simple for greater
success.

7:28

SELF-CONTROL IS CRITICAL IF YOU WANT TO
reach your goal (Philippians 3:12,14).

7:29

Chapter 7

7:30   IT'S IMPORTANT TO BUILD TIME INTO YOUR regular routine to prep for the next step.

7:31   A SERVANT LEADER IS A PERSON WITH THE seemingly contradictory qualities of being bold and humble, egoless and empowering, and credit worthy and credit giving.

Chapter 8

Don't let your deliberation defer 8:1 _____
you from your ultimate destination.

A menial task can become a meaningful 8:2 _____
task if you approach it with the right attitude and give
it your best.

A paradox of servant leadership is that 8:3 _____
giving of yourself is both draining and fulfilling.

Be generous with your time and 8:4 _____
resources to meet others' needs.

Chapter 8

8:5   YOU CAN USUALLY ATTRIBUTE THE QUALITY of leaders attracted to an organization to the quality of leaders leading the organization.

8:6   CREATE A DREAM JOB FOR SOMEONE BY setting clear goals, giving adequate authority and providing appropriate resources.

8:7   CONTEMPLATE YOUR COMPLIMENTS BEFORE you communicate them. Be specific and sincere.

8:8   BE COMFORTABLE, NOT COMPLACENT, IN YOUR leadership.

LEADERS DON'T SHUN PROBLEMS; THEY SOLVE   8:9
them.

YOU'LL IMPRESS OTHERS IF YOU HANDLE   8:10
pressure well. Inspire confidence by keeping your
cool.

IF YOUR FOLLOWERS AREN'T IMITATING YOUR   8:11
leadership style, you need to change it.

WHEN SUCCESS COMES, GIVE THE CREDIT TO   8:12
your team. You will gain loyalty, productivity
and appreciation, and, as a bonus, the credit will
boomerang back to you.

Chapter 8

8:13   SERVANT LEADERSHIP IS NOT ABOUT GAINING power, it is about earning respect and authority.

8:14   HAVING A GOOD NAME IS MUCH BETTER THAN having a big name (Proverbs 22:1).

8:15   A SMALL COSMETIC CHANGE IN THE OFFICE can increase team morale and first impressions. Create an atmosphere of excellence and beauty.

8:16   YOUR DISPOSITION ABOUT LIFE CAN ENABLE or disable your opportunities to obtain a leadership position.

A RIGHT HEART WILL HELP YOU MAKE THE   8:17
right decisions every time.

⁂

DON'T LEAVE THINGS UP TO CHANCE OR   8:18
circumstance. Plan ahead.

⁂

GIVE IT YOUR BEST, AND THE REST WILL   8:19
usually take care of itself.

⁂

DON'T LET YOUR VISION FADE. IF YOU DON'T   8:20
know where you are going, no one will follow you.

Chapter 8

8:21   THE INFANCY STAGE OF AN IDEA REQUIRES the greatest infusion of expertise and energy.

8:22   A TRUE LEADER WILL SHINE WHEN everything is on the line. Step up, not aside, during those moments.

8:23   SERVANT LEADERS ARE COMMITTED TO THE growth of those they lead as much as they are committed to the growth of the organization.

8:24   REFERENCE YOUR PREFERENCE WHEN possible, then your team will make the right decision in your absence.

SOMETIMES SIMPLY SURVIVING IS SUCCESS.   8:25
Keep difficult times in perspective.

LEAVE YOUR MARK ON YOUR ORGANIZATION   8:26
by leaving it in better shape when you depart than
when you embarked as its leader. Don't leave things
in shambles for your successor.

INTERVENE WHEN THERE ARE INTERRUPTIONS   8:27
during a meeting. Keep things moving.

REFRAIN FROM SAYING ANYTHING YOU WOULD   8:28
not want reported or repeated outside of the meeting.

Chapter 8

8:29   AS A GENERAL RULE OF THUMB, STAY OUT OF it unless you are willing to be stuck in it.

8:30   MENTORING IS MOST EFFECTIVE WHEN IT IS relational, intentional and motivational.

Chapter 9

WITH DISCIPLINE, FOCUS AND
determination, your daily DO list can
become a daily DONE list.

9:1 _____

LEADERS NEED TO BE MORE THAN CONVINCED
that something is true, they need to effectively
communicate their conviction.

9:2 _____

RESPECT IS AN IMPORTANT ASPECT OF
leadership. Don't risk losing it when you receive it. It's
always easier to maintain than to regain.

9:3 _____

ALWAYS RESERVE FINAL JUDGMENT UNTIL YOU
have all the necessary information.

9:4 _____

Chapter 9

9:5 SERVANT LEADERS GIVE GRACE GENEROUSLY to team members endeavoring to improve. They build people, not just the organization.

9:6 HAVING TALENT IS INSUFFICIENT IF YOU don't implement and improve your abilities over time (2 Timothy 1:6).

9:7 NEVER MAKE AN ACCUSATION WITHOUT complete and accurate information (1 Timothy 5:19).

9:8 IT'S SAD WHEN YOU AREN'T GLAD ABOUT someone else's success (Romans 12:15).

THINGS THAT ARE WORTHWHILE TAKE A
while to achieve. Be patient.

9:9 _____

BE PRECISE AND CONCISE WHEN YOU GIVE
advice. Repeat as necessary.

9:10 _____

CAREFULLY CHART A SMART START BEFORE
implementing your next idea.

9:11 _____

YOU HAVE TO SACRIFICE FOR LEADERSHIP
success. You must pay ahead to get ahead.

9:12 _____

Chapter 9

9:13   WHEN YOU LEAVE YOUR LEADERSHIP UP TO luck, you're stuck. Don't gamble your fortune or your future.

9:14   NATURAL ABILITY DOES NOT GUARANTEE advancement; using it with regularity and dexterity does.

9:15   DON'T WAIT UNTIL THE FINAL INNING OF your life to thank God for His blessings given to you and through you.

9:16   WHEN YOU ACKNOWLEDGE GOD'S GOODNESS in your life, you give glory where glory is due.

HAVING LIBERTY DOES NOT LIBERATE YOU
from responsibility.

9:17 _____

YOUR LEADERSHIP APPROACH WILL MAKE
your leadership efforts appealing or appalling.

9:18 _____

SEVERING A TIE WITH SOMEONE CAN HAVE
severe consequences. Consider alternate solutions
first. Don't burn a bridge unless there is no other way
across.

9:19 _____

LEADERS WHO HAVE RUINED THEIR
reputation find that the restoration of their reputation
is a long and painful process.

9:20 _____

9:21　SERVANT LEADERS NEED TO BE CAREFUL
their words don't contain a self-righteous bias.

9:22　GIVE YOUR COMPLIMENTS GENEROUSLY AND
your complaints sparingly.

9:23　A LEADER CANNOT AFFORD TO BE
indifferent toward danger indicators.

9:24　SUCCESS HAS ITS DANGERS. SOME WILL TEAR
you down and others will want to give you so much
work that it will weigh you down. Fight the first and
flee the second.

BE ANIMATED FROM TIME TO TIME WITHOUT
being automated. Be passionate without being
predictable.

9:25 _____

DON'T DISTORT YOUR REPORT. IF IT'S BAD,
tell it like it is. If it's good, don't embellish or
exaggerate it.

9:26 _____

FIND CREATIVE WAYS TO ADD HUMOR INTO
the workplace. Laughter lightens everybody's load.

9:27 _____

DON'T TIP OVER. FIND BALANCE IN YOUR
life.

9:28 _____

Chapter 9

9:29   IT IS WISE TO HAVE A TRUSTED CONFIDANT
outside your organization to ease your burdens and
strengthen your soul. Leadership can be a heavy
weight to bear.

9:30   AUTHENTIC SERVANTS ARE NOT WORRIED
about their individual reputations. That will take care
of itself.

9:31

SOMETIMES YOU HAVE TO GET MOVING TO
start improving. If you don't, you'll never get started.

Chapter 10

THE GOAL OF A GREAT LEADER IS NOT TO reach the target first but for the team to reach it together.

10:1

USE YOUR POWER AND INFLUENCE TO protect your people. Sacrifice yourself to be their shield.

10:2

AN OUTSTANDING LEADER DOESN'T CARRY the vision alone—the entire team owns it.

10:3

COMMIT TO YOUR MISSION SO COMPLETELY that it will outlast your leadership.

10:4

Chapter 10

10:5   ONE OF THE BEST WAYS TO INSPIRE A TEAM member is to take some time to understand and admire their work.

10:6   IT'S DIFFICULT TO OVERCOME LIFE'S obstacles when you feel completely overwhelmed. Trust God and take them on one day at a time.

10:7   IT'S YOUR ACTIONS, NOT YOUR ARGUMENTS, that will help you advance to a successful solution.

10:8   THE DECISIONS YOU MAKE IN LIFE WILL MAKE you. Mess them up and you can miss some great opportunities.

SERVANT LEADERS GIVE REGULAR   10:9
supervision to their direct reports to help make them
successful.

WISE LEADERS ARE METICULOUS IN THEIR   10:10
decision-making processes.

TAILGATE WHAT YOU DELEGATE. FOLLOW UP   10:11
on assignments and responsibilities you entrusted to
your team.

GO THE SECOND MILE. YOU WILL FIND IT   10:12
worth your while (Matthew 5:41).

Chapter 10

10:13   TIME HAS A TENDENCY TO CLARIFY AND
verify the truth. Sometimes it is wise to delay until
you can discern.

10:14   RIGHT CHARACTER IS THE KEY TO RIGHT
conduct.

10:15   DEVELOP YOUR VIRTUES OR YOU WILL
default to vices.

10:16   IF YOU ASK SOMEONE TO DO SOMETHING AND
they don't act, find another method of motivation.

YOU MUST BUILD RAPPORT BEFORE YOU CAN restore a broken relationship.

10:17

TAKE ADVANTAGE OF DIVERSE ADVICE BEFORE making difficult decisions.

10:18

YOU CAN SKEW YOUR UNDERSTANDING OF information if you only look at it from your own point of view.

10:19

REFUSE TO OVERUSE AN EXCUSE. THAT CAN become habit forming.

10:20

Chapter 10

10:21   INSECURE PEOPLE BRAG ABOUT THEMSELVES.

10:22   SERVANT LEADERSHIP AND SELF-SACRIFICE generate a generational effect. You will have influence long after you are gone.

10:23   IF IT IS NOT SCARY, IT IS NOT AN AUDACIOUS goal. Buttress your courage, take a step of faith, work hard and trust God for the results.

10:24   A VERBAL PROCLAMATION IS NOT AS productive as a visual demonstration. Remember, actions speak louder than words.

SUCCESS IS MAGNETIC. COMBINE IT WITH A greater vision and it will attract other leaders to your cause.

10:25

TAKE TIME TO ENGINEER OPPORTUNITIES TO volunteer with your organization. You can exponentially increase your leadership impact.

10:26

CREATE THE RIGHT WORK ATMOSPHERE AND the right workers will adhere to your organization.

10:27

NEVER LET IT APPEAR THAT YOU DON'T OBEY your own rules or policies. No one wants to follow a hypocritical leader.

10:28

Chapter 10

10:29 YOUR LEADERSHIP CAN BE DESTROYED IF YOU constantly or inappropriately avoid difficult conversations and confrontations.

10:30 SERVANT LEADERS ARE ON AN EDUCATIONAL expedition, always exploring something new and teaching it to their team.

10:31 IT'S IMPORTANT FOR LEADERS TO AVOID A silo and solo mentality toward the team.

Chapter 11

PUT POLICIES IN PLACE AND THEN POLICE them from time to time. Just because they were documented does not mean they are being implemented.

11:1

YOUR POLICIES SHOULD BE EASILY retrievable and reviewable. Put them in a manual and review them annually.

11:2

DON'T PUNISH THE ENTIRE GROUP FOR AN ongoing problem with one person. Use a bullet, not a shotgun, or you will injure bystanders.

11:3

SERVANT LEADERS AREN'T LOUD OR PROUD, but they still get the job done. The best advice you can receive is to stay humble.

11:4

Chapter 11

11:5 YOUR TITLE MAY ENTITLE YOU TO RULE, BUT
it is no guarantee you can lead. People won't thrive
if you only drive them. Positional power alone won't
take you far.

11:6 A SMART LEADER WILL ALWAYS TURN A
challenging moment into an opportunity to learn
something.

11:7 IT IS THE LEADER'S RESPONSIBILITY TO BE
the glue between continuity and change.

11:8 PEOPLE CAN BE WELL MEANING AND APPEAR
to be mean at the same time. Expect it and be
prepared to overlook their honest offense.

YOUR PERSONNEL WILL NEVER DO THEIR BEST   11:9
if you are not giving your personal best in everything
you do. Lead by example.

YOU DON'T HAVE TO SOUND MEAN FOR YOUR   11:10
team to know you mean what you say.

ANYTIME A LEADER ADDS VALUE BY GIVING   11:11
input, they increase their level of influence and
impact.

IF YOU ONLY RIDE THE WAVE OF YOUR   11:12
predecessor's success, it will finally peter out and
leave you stranded.

Chapter 11

11:13   YOU HAVE TO TAKE FULL RESPONSIBILITY FOR what happens under your leadership watch. Servant leaders bounce the credit they get for success right back to their staff, which generates even more effort.

11:14   AS A LEADER, YOU HAVE TO TACKLE TOUGH situations with a great deal of tact, or you will cause a great deal of trauma or trouble.

11:15   DON'T LET THE MESSAGE YOU NEED TO convey get lost because you lose your temper.

11:16   IMPROVEMENT IS WELL DEFINED AS THE "expansion of excellence." Continually increase your borders.

YOU HAVE TO LEARN HOW TO MANAGE
moments of defeat and disappointment or, like a
broken leg, they will hinder your ability to lead on
your long journey.

11:17

MAKE "CUSTOMER CARE" MANDATORY WITHIN
your organization. Customize a process to make your
customers feel valued and appreciated.

11:18

THE REAL VALUE OF A VOLUNTEER IS NOT
based on the volume of work they produce but the
devotion with which they perform it.

11:19

SET ASIDE TIME EVERY YEAR TO RECOGNIZE
and honor the people who volunteer within your
organization.

11:20

Chapter 11

11:21   PEOPLE LOVE WORKING FOR A SERVANT leader because they give rise to an excellent corporate culture. Staff retention is remarkable.

11:22   TAKE A MOMENT TO WRITE A PERSONAL NOTE of appreciation. The recipient can share it and reread it from time to time.

11:23   ANYTIME YOU DEMONSTRATE THE SKILL TO design and administrate an effective strategy, you add to the trust of your team.

11:24   IT IS DIFFICULT TO COMPETE WITH OBSOLETE information. Stay current and up to date.

TEACH RESPONSIBILITY THROUGH 11:25
accountability. What gets measured gets done.

WHEN YOUR HEART IS BROKEN IN 11:26
leadership, you can let it ache or let it act. Don't delay
to address the issue.

YOU MAY LEAVE YOUR LEADERSHIP POSITION, 11:27
but your good or bad impression will linger long after
you are gone.

DON'T DISENGAGE OVER A DISAPPOINTMENT. 11:28
Renew and refocus your efforts.

Chapter 11

11:29   PERIODICALLY STEP ASIDE AND TAKE A
break. It can keep you from permanently walking
away.

11:30   IT IS THE LEADER'S RESPONSIBILITY TO HEAL
the gripes handicapping their team.

Chapter 12

YOU ARE NOT ALONE, EVEN THOUGH leadership can be lonely. Find a peer, a mentor or another person in your executive team to be a confidant in your leadership journey.

12:1

IT'S IMPORTANT FOR A LEADER TO FORGIVE, forget and move forward. Anger will strand you in the past. Strive on to the future.

12:2

EVEN GOOD THINGS COME TO A PROPER END. A leader has the wit to know when it's time to quit and move on.

12:3

A LEADER HAS TO GET ENOUGH SLEEP TO BE fresh and focused. Resolve to rest and establish a good routine.

12:4

Chapter 12

12:5   DON'T LET IT TAKE A SERIES OF SERIOUS situations to motivate you to take something or someone seriously.

12:6   YOU WILL PAY IF YOU DELAY, SO DON'T dawdle until the task is complete. Get the job done.

12:7   GETTING YOUR NEW INITIATIVES DONE efficiently and proficiently will give you a competitive advantage over your competition.

12:8   LEADERS ARE ABLE TO OBTAIN AND MAINTAIN excellence through constant evaluation and enhancement.

YOUR OPPOSITION EXPLOITS OPPORTUNITIES. Don't give them any.

12:9

ANY TIME YOU SERVE ON A TEAM, WORK TO complete and complement the group. Be the oil in the gears.

12:10

AN ENTREPRENEURIAL LEADER WOULD rather make something out of nothing than try to tweak the status quo. They will always choose the challenge over the comfortable.

12:11

WHENEVER WE BECOME DISTRACTED, OUR vision becomes distorted.

12:12

Chapter 12

12:13   CAREFULLY AND METHODICALLY EXTRACT anything distracting you from carrying out your mission (Matthew 18:8).

12:14   PEACE AND HARMONY ARE THE REWARDS FOR overcoming difficult situations. Be smart. Deal with problems when they are still small.

12:15   ACTIONS AUTHENTICATE YOUR WORDS— tightly link them.

12:16   YOU CAN'T BUILD A STRONG ORGANIZATION on a weak governance foundation. Liberally spend your time in strengthening your board.

IT'S OBVIOUS WE SHOULD AVOID EVIL THAT IS apparent, but we should also avoid even the very appearance of evil (1 Thessalonians 5:22).

12:17

MOST ORGANIZATIONS CAN'T AFFORD ALL the salaried staff they need, so leaders need to regularly recruit, recognize and reward their volunteers in order to retain them.

12:18

DO SOMETHING TODAY FOR THOSE WHO CAN never repay you. As a servant leader, execute acts of kindness expecting absolutely nothing in return. You will be better for it (Luke 6:35-38).

12:19

IT'S ESSENTIAL FOR SUCCESS THAT EVERY non-profit organization engineer an effective volunteer program.

12:20

Chapter 12

12:21   RESPECT THE VARIOUS PERSPECTIVES ON your team. Thank God that others are not all just like you!

12:22   IT'S IMPORTANT FOR A LEADER TO ALWAYS keep an "improvement list." There is a better way to do everything. Find it!

12:23   YOUR BOARD MEMBERS SHOULD HAVE THE skills, expertise, connections and servant hearts necessary to wisely craft the mission, vision, goals and policies of your organization.

12:24   SOME LEADERS HAVE THE GIFT TO INSPIRE IN others a desire for greatness. If you have that gift, use it for good.

MANAGEMENT BY MANIPULATION IS
leadership malpractice.

12:25

SERVANT LEADERS WILLFULLY SUBMIT TO
their governance body. Unaccountable leaders are
hazardous to themselves and their organization.

12:26

TRUE SUCCESS IS A SUCCESSION OF ACTS OF
obedience to God. Follow His will faithfully
throughout your entire life.

12:27

HIRE PEOPLE SMARTER THAN YOU. INVEST IN
their success. Mentor them to greatness.

12:28

Chapter 12

12:29   IN PUBLIC SPEAKING, YOU HAVE TO READ
your audience before you can reach your audience.

12:30   PRIDE IS NEVER PRETTY. GET THE UGLY OUT
of your life before it hurts you (Proverbs 16:18).

12:31   ACTION AND ACCOMPLISHMENT ARE THE
differences between a dreamer and a daydreamer.

Chapter 13

TO GENERATE A LASTING LEGACY, INVEST your life and leadership in the next generation.

DO NOT DIMINISH YOUR LEVEL OF ENERGY and enthusiasm for what you're doing until you're finished.

13:2

TAKE A MOMENT TO REFLECT ON THE LESSONS you've learned during the day and you'll never neglect to benefit from the wisdom you've gained.

13:3

SOME OF LIFE'S MOST REWARDING experiences come from things for which we weren't reimbursed.

13:4

Chapter 13

13:5   LIFELONG LEADERS PACE THEMSELVES throughout their race. The trophy is not won by one trip around the track.

13:6   EVERY ENDING CAN BE A NEW BEGINNING. Perceive it from that perspective.

13:7   FEAR DOES NOT EQUAL RESPECT. YOU WILL BE admired for who you are, not for your power.

13:8   PRESS ON WHEN THE PRESSURE IS ON. LET IT mold you into something better and not break you.

SERVANT LEADERS DO MORE THAN LEAD, THEY 13:9
minister to their followers to help them become all
God designed them to be.

IMPROVEMENT IS A MEASURABLE PROOF OF 13:10
progress.

PURSUE PATIENCE UNTIL IT BECOMES A 13:11
virtue of your leadership.

BOARDS SHOULD ERECT POLICY FENCES 13:12
around their leadership to tell them what they can't
do, not what they can do. "Mother may I?" boards
hamstring their leaders.

Chapter 13

13:13 AN ORGANIZATIONAL VISION STATEMENT IS
not a slogan. It describes what it will look like when
you accomplish your mission.

13:14 AFTER YOU AND YOUR BOARD AGREE ON YOUR
organization's goals and available financial resources,
it is the leader's job to develop and execute the
strategy to get there.

13:15 IT'S ALWAYS EASIER TO CRITIQUE THAN TO
create.

13:16 TRIUMPHS AND DISAPPOINTMENTS ARE
temporary. Keep an eternal perspective.

FOLLOWERS EVENTUALLY VACATE THE TEAM
when there is a vacuum of leadership.

13:17

IT IS YOUR BOARD'S JOB TO HIRE, EVALUATE,
compensate, motivate and, if necessary, fire you, the
leader. Their job is to make sure you stay on mission,
but it is your job to accomplish it.

13:18

IT IS YOUR JOB TO HIRE, EVALUATE,
compensate, motivate and, if necessary, fire each
of your employees. You employ them to help you
accomplish your organization's mission.

13:19

CONFIDENCE COMES BY MAKING SENSIBLE
decisions based on the right application of knowledge
and experience.

13:20

Chapter 13

13:21   NEVER HIRE SOMEONE WHO LACKS
character. You can't teach character like you can teach
competence.

13:22   DON'T SIMPLY HIRE YOUR STAFF, ADOPT THEM
into your organization's family. You are not offering
them a job but a relationship.

13:23   THERE ARE THREE LEVELS OF OBSERVATION:

- ⟿ Blind observation (does not see anything).

- ⟿ Biased observation (sees things from one point of
  view).

- ⟿ Balanced observation (looks at things objectively
  from every point of view possible).

SERVANT LEADERS HAVE DECIDED THEY WILL   13:24
lead for the benefit of others, not to increase their
own power, prestige or wealth.

BEFORE ADOPTING A NEW TEAM MEMBER,   13:25
make sure the chemistry is right. It only takes one
rotten banana to spoil the entire bunch.

CREATE CLEAR AND CONCISE WRITTEN   13:26
standards of performance for each of your team
members. Those standards tell you and them when
they are meeting your expectations.

DON'T HAVE FAVORITES, BUT DO BE FRIENDS   13:27
with each of your staff members. They can love you
as a friend and respect you as their boss at the same
time.

Chapter 13

13:28   THERE IS LITTLE REWARD WITHOUT RISK, BUT the job of the leader is to take the minimum risk necessary to get the maximum results.

13:29   IF YOU THINK SUCCESS IS A PIE, YOU WILL compete to make your piece bigger by making others' pieces smaller. In reality, success is a bottomless well. Share the secrets of your success with others—it is like giving a cup of water to a thirsty man.

13:30   CHERISH THE PRECIOUS MOMENTS THAT PASS quickly in life. Don't let your purpose-driven personality take precedence over life's special moments.

13:31   ALWAYS DO WHAT IS RIGHT IN SPITE OF WHAT everyone else is doing.

Chapter 14

DELIBERATE, DEBATE AND THEN DEFEND   14:1
your decisions with your team in unity.

THERE ARE FOUR TYPES OF POWER: COERCIVE,   14:2
manipulative, persuasive and influential. Servant
leadership influences people to give their utmost for
the benefit of others.

ASK PROSPECTIVE STAFF THIS REVEALING   14:3
question: "Is there anything in your background
that, if it came to light, would embarrass you or this
organization?"

EMPOWER YOUR TEAM BY GIVING THEM   14:4
clear objectives, fixed deadlines, adequate resources
and enough authority to be successful—and then
cheer them on.

Chapter 14

14:5   IF YOU LEAD A CHRISTIAN ORGANIZATION, publicly pray and worship as a team. As you draw closer to Christ, you will draw closer to each other.

14:6   SEEK ADVICE FROM PEOPLE WHO HAVE already done what you want to do. Grasp useful ideas. Improve them and apply them. You don't need to recreate the wheel.

14:7   LIKE OVEREATING, OVERWORKING WILL KILL your joy, your health and you.

14:8   ONE COURAGEOUS ACT CAN ALTER THE future for years to come. Be audacious.

RESULTS DON'T LIE. DON'T EMBELLISH THE truth.   14:9

A GOOD SIGN SOMEONE IS READY FOR leadership is when they take every assignment seriously, projecting their very best into every project.   14:10

MODELING A BEHAVIOR IS ALWAYS MORE effective than mandating a behavior.   14:11

STRATEGIC PLANNING STARTS WITH strategic thinking. Do an environmental scan, understand your constituents' needs, imagine innovative solutions and then set concrete goals.   14:12

Chapter 14

14:13   NOT EVERY GOOD IDEA IS A STRATEGIC IDEA.
It has to move you forward in accomplishing your
mission.

14:14   STRATEGIC PLANNING IS STRENUOUS WORK.
That is why you need a strong group to accomplish it.

14:15   MOVEMENT CREATES MOMENTUM. DEVELOP A
plan to get things moving in the right direction.

14:16   THE ONLY THING SAFE TO ASSUME IN
leadership is responsibility. Don't pass the buck.

SOME PEOPLE USE THEIR CIRCUMSTANCES TO   14:17
make excuses. Leaders act to change their
circumstances.

TALENT CAN BE BURIED OR BROADENED,   14:18
curtailed or cultivated.

CREATE A WORKING ENVIRONMENT TO   14:19
stimulate, not frustrate, innovative thinking.

SERVANT LEADERS BENEFIT FROM OTHERS   14:20
sharing information, contacts and insights. It makes
them more effective.

Chapter 14

14:21   A LACK OF ADEQUATE COMPENSATION demotivates your staff, but you can't motivate people with just money for long. Lasting motivation comes from being recognized for accomplishing something worthwhile with their talents.

14:22   YOUR SUCCESS IN LIFE HAS MORE TO DO WITH the choices you make than the circumstances thrust upon you. Choose wisely.

14:23   SUCCESS HAS A PRICE TAG. IT'S CALLED sacrifice.

14:24   LACK OF OPPORTUNITY CAN BE YOUR greatest opponent. Seek opportunities (Philippians 4:10).

A LEADER CAN TOLERATE DIFFERENCES OF opinion, but never division.

14:25

∗

YOU HAVE ENOUGH INFORMATION WHEN YOU accumulate enough to make a wise decision.

14:26

∗

POWER CAN EITHER GO TO YOUR HEAD IN pride or go into your hands to help.

14:27

∗

SERVANT LEADERS ARE NOT THREATENED BY people who are more talented than they are. They are going to give away any credit coming their way anyway.

14:28

Chapter 14

14:29   DON'T BE TOO PREDICTABLE WHEN IT COMES
to having fun with your staff. Surprise them in
creative ways to let off steam and reinvigorate their
productivity.

14:30   A LEADER'S DECISION-MAKING HAS TO BE
decisive without being divisive.

14:31   LEADERS DON'T GIVE UP. THEY GET UP AND
keep moving.

Chapter 15

C AREFULLY WEIGH THE OPTIONS BEFORE 15:1
you weigh in and offer your opinion.

IF YOU HAVE A CONFLICT WITH ONE OF YOUR 15:2
staff members and are unsuccessful in solving or
settling it, you may need to dismiss them.

AS THE CAPTAIN OF THE SHIP, IT'S YOUR 15:3
responsibility to renew your crew.

DON'T JUST CHART THE COURSE YOU PLAN TO 15:4
pursue. Captain the voyage to your destination.

15:5   SERVANT LEADERS ARE LIKE PHYSICIANS.
They recognize each team member's weaknesses and
work to make them whole.

* * *

15:6   DO NOT LET A MISTAKE YOU MAKE CONTINUE
to take advantage of you. Confess, apologize, learn
and then head in the right direction.

* * *

15:7   YOU CANNOT DELEGATE YOUR DECISION
disasters to someone else. Clean up your own messes.

* * *

15:8   WHEN YOU PROTECT PEOPLE FROM
experiencing painful consequences, you prevent them
from profiting from that experience.

BE MERCIFUL WHEN PEOPLE OCCASIONALLY   15:9
mess up. You will likely need the same favor.

SOMETIMES IT IS WISE TO GIVE IN A BIT TO   15:10
get what you want. A good compromise can be a
win-win.

DON'T LET PROBLEMS GROW. LIKE WEEDS,   15:11
they are easiest to handle when they are small.

"HAPPY TALK" WILL NOT HIDE YOUR   15:12
dilemma. It is like wrapping a cow pie in gift paper. It
still stinks.

Chapter 15

15:13   APPROPRIATELY VACATE YOUR
responsibilities when you go on vacation. Accomplish
the urgent and delegate the rest. If you can't mentally
leave, physically leaving won't restore you.

15:14   WISE ADVICE IS INVALUABLE. YOU DON'T
have enough time or resources not to seek it.

15:15   A NEGATIVE LEADER WILL NEVER MAKE A
positive impact on the organization.

15:16   SERVANT LEADERS EMPATHIZE. THEY
understand people, so they are able to take them from
where they are toward where they need to be.

IT'S FOOLISH TO MAKE A FINAL DECISION ON 15:17
a matter without having adequate knowledge of all
the facts and options available.

HARD DECISIONS RARELY MAKE EVERYONE 15:18
happy. Leaders have the courage to make them
anyway.

YOUR TEAM IS MORE LIKELY TO BELIEVE IN 15:19
themselves when they know you believe in them.

YOUR DRIVE AS A LEADER WILL ENABLE YOU 15:20
to arrive at your dreams. Dreams detached from your
drive go nowhere.

Chapter 15

15:21   BE FIRM WITH WHAT MATTERS MOST. BE flexible in matters with little consequences.

15:22   PROVE YOUR PURSUIT OF EXCELLENCE BY proofing everything you do.

15:23   YOU NEVER REALLY SOLVE A PROBLEM without involving everyone affected.

15:24   REMEMBER THAT ALL COMPLAINTS ARE NOT without cause. Ignore the petty but tackle the valid ones.

SOMETIMES THE MOST EFFECTIVE THING YOU can say is NOTHING. You can silence your critics with quiet.

15:25

ONE PIECE OF INSIGHTFUL ADVICE CAN markedly advance your cause. Pay attention and heed.

15:26

A DEPENDABLE LEADER IS EASY TO DEFEND.

15:27

YOU CAN STILL STRIKE OUT EVEN IF YOU don't swing the bat.

15:28

Chapter 15

15:29   BUILD YOUR TEAM TO BUILD YOUR
organization.

15:30   SERVANTS LISTEN WELL TO UNDERSTAND AND
do the right thing. So do servant leaders.

15:31   A LEADER SHOULD CORRESPOND
immediately even if they can't respond immediately.
In your correspondence, let them know you received
the information and then set the expectation of when
you will be able to take action on it.

Chapter 16

HINDSIGHT CAN GIVE YOU GREAT insight and also sharpen your foresight.

16:1

WISE LEADERS NEITHER ELEVATE NOR belittle themselves in the eyes of their employees.

16:2

IN YOUR ATTEMPT TO BE AGGRESSIVE AS A leader, don't trample on people.

16:3

TIME CAN CERTAINLY REVEAL YOUR leadership reputation, but it will not necessarily repeal it.

16:4

Chapter 16

16:5   THERE ARE TWO KINDS OF PEOPLE WHEN IT comes to burdens in leadership: burden casters (Luke 11:46) and burden bearers (Galatians 6:2).

16:6   YOU WILL HAVE LEADERSHIP BURNOUT IF YOU don't continually add fuel to your passion fire.

16:7   SERVANT LEADERS HAVE A LOW LEVEL OF control over their team, so picking the right team members is essential. Seek those with the right character, chemistry and common sense who are humble and hungry to succeed.

16:8   OUR WORLD DOESN'T NEED MORE EXCUSES. IT needs more dynamic leaders.

NO MATTER HOW BAD THE SITUATION, GOOD 16:9
leaders figure out the right direction, head there and
take others with them.

A LEADER HAS TO KNOW WHEN TO OVERLOOK, 16:10
when to overturn and when to overhaul.

CHASE YOUR DREAMS BY CHARTING A 16:11
specific course to the preferred destination. Set sail!

A CARING LEADER KNOWS HOW TO APPLY 16:12
correction with the seasoning of affection.

Chapter 16

16:13   IF YOU ARE OFFENSIVE IN YOUR ACTIONS, others will be defensive in their reactions.

16:14   FORCE MAY WIN A BATTLE, BUT WINSOMENESS wins the war.

16:15   PACE YOURSELF IN THE RACE YOU ARE running so you don't fall down or drop out.

16:16   YOUR MOTHER TOLD YOU, "GOOD MANNERS matter." That was true then, and it is especially true now that you're a leader.

MEASURE AND TEST YOUR SUCCESS BY WHAT 16:17
you treasure. It should be the people you've
developed, not the power, position or money you've
obtained.

IF YOU GO OVER PEOPLE'S HEADS, YOU MAY 16:18
get yours chopped off. Use the proper channels.

FOLLOW THROUGH IS WHAT YOU DO WHEN 16:19
you are an effective leader.

THE MOST EFFECTIVE FORM OF TRAINING IS 16:20
apprenticeship. Invest your leadership capital there.

Chapter 16

16:21   DON'T OVERCOMMIT TO YOUR METHOD TO the expense of your mission.

16:22   SUCCESS DOES NOT ALWAYS EQUATE TO satisfaction.

16:23   IT IS NOT THE CAPTAIN'S JOB TO BAIL THE boat but to steer the ship. Stay on task.

16:24   FAITHFUL LEADERS WILL NOT ONLY GIVE their word but also live out their word. Complete what you communicate.

SERVANT LEADERS INSPIRE THEIR FOLLOWERS
to reach their highest potential because they aspire to
model themselves after them.

16:25

REAL CHANGE REQUIRES YOU TO REARRANGE
the roles and responsibilities of your team. You can't
reset your course without resetting your sails.

16:26

PERSONAL DISCIPLINE LARGELY DETERMINES
success. Practice it yourself. Demand it from your
team members.

16:27

FUEL YOUR PASSION UNTIL IT LIGHTS YOUR
team on fire to accomplish your cause.

16:28

Chapter 16

16:29   IF YOU DON'T TRUST A TEAM MEMBER, IT IS time to lose that team member. It is not good for you or them to continue the relationship.

16:30   SERVANT LEADERSHIP IS TURNING THE typical organizational hierarchy upside down. Serve your people instead of expecting them to serve you.

16:31   LEADERS DON'T WASTE TIME FUSSING ABOUT things they are not able to fix.

Chapter 17

Don't waste your time or others' time. Don't imply interest in an offer when you have no intention of giving a positive reply.

17:1

Carefully review a written communication before responding to it. Skimming documents predisposes you to costly errors.

17:2

Intuition is a leader's early warning system to prevent organizational damage. Develop yours or link to a trusted team member who has it.

17:3

Every leader will be judged by their "doing:" not enough, just enough or more than enough.

17:4

Chapter 17

17:5 A LEADER WILL BE REMEMBERED BY WHAT they DID and DIDN'T do.

✳

17:6 A SERVANT LEADER'S RESPONSIBILITY IS TO help all employees become the best version of themselves, not only at work, but at home and in their communities.

✳

17:7 EFFECTIVE LEADERSHIP IS NOT A SPRINT BUT an endurance race. Stay the course until you finish the course.

✳

17:8 GREAT LEADERS ARE FIRST GREAT FOLLOWERS (Matthew 4:19).

YOU CAN OFTEN OVERCOME RESISTANCE WITH persistence. Be tenacious.

17:9

∗

GOD TREASURES PEOPLE AND HAS ENTRUSTED people to you. Your stewardship mandate is to develop them.

17:10

∗

NOT EVERY GOOD OPPORTUNITY IS FROM God. Wisely examine them and your motives before you act.

17:11

∗

A LEADER HAS TO MAKE A DECISION BECAUSE it is the right thing to do, not because the right people want it done.

17:12

Chapter 17

17:13   CLEAR COMMUNICATION REDUCES LOW LEVEL
discontent caused by poorly explained decisions.

※

17:14   YOUR TEAM NEEDS TO KNOW WHERE YOU
want them to go and how they're doing in getting
there. Evaluate their performance regularly.

※

17:15   A LEADER MUST HAVE INTEGRITY. JUST
because everyone is doing it does not make it right.

※

17:16   WHAT LEGACY DO YOU WANT TO LEAVE?
Adjust your priorities so what you wish will become
so.

BE CAREFUL HOW YOU FORCE A COURSE 17:17
correction: too fast and you will capsize; too slow and
you won't reach your destination.

AVOID CHANGE OVERLOAD. DISCERN THE 17:18
difference between the decisions that must be made
today and the ones that can wait until tomorrow.

IF YOUR LOAD IS TOO HEAVY, YOU CAN'T GO 17:19
anywhere. Shed the unimportant, the untimely and
what others can do.

SERVANT LEADERS BELIEVE EVERY PERSON 17:20
has inestimable value, so they extend them courtesy,
honor and respect.

Chapter 17

17:21　YOU ONLY HAVE SO MUCH ENERGY TO SHARE. When you give some to something new, you take it from somewhere else.

17:22　POSSESSION PRINCIPLES:

- ◆ (1)　Honor God with what you have.

- ◆ (2)　Be content with what you have.

- ◆ (3)　Make the most of what you have.

- ◆ (4)　Take good care of what you have.

- ◆ (5)　Share what you have.

17:23　IN WORK AND PLAY, DO YOURSELF AND others a favor by adding a different flavor from time to time. Variety truly is the spice of life.

YOU STYMIE PROGRESS AND CREATIVITY   17:24
when you allow tradition to be the trump card.
Release the reins and let the race horses on your team
run.

A BOSS DOES NOT HAVE TO BE BOSSY.   17:25

CONSISTENTLY COMMUNICATE YOUR VALUES   17:26
to your team. Let them know what behavior you
expect as they pursue your mission.

A PLAN ACCOMPLISHES NO PURPOSE UNLESS   17:27
you fuel it with fervor and then execute your strategy.

Chapter 17

17:28   SERVANT LEADERS ENCOURAGE OTHERS TO DO
         what they do—set aside self-serving behaviors.

17:29   CLEAR EXPECTATIONS ENSURE QUALITY
         outcomes.

17:30   ROLL WITH THE THINGS THAT ARE OUT OF
         your leadership control.

Chapter 18

WEAK LEADERSHIP EXPLAINS THE current state of numerous organizations. You can't build a strong organization on a weak foundation.

18:1

COURTESY IS BASIC DECENCY. HOSPITALITY goes further because you give generously of your time and resources to make someone feel welcome.

18:2

TO AVOID DISGRACE, BE ACCURATE IN WHAT you articulate.

18:3

A SERVANT LEADERSHIP STYLE WILL CAUSE your team members to flourish and not famish. It won't cause frustration but will bear the fruit of progress.

18:4

Chapter 18

18:5   A GOOD DIET OF QUIET IS HEALTHY FOR A
stressed or distressed leader.

18:6   THE COST OF CONCEALING A MATTER IS FAR
greater than being open and honest in confessing that
issue to others.

18:7   THE BEST WAY TO MEET THE NEEDS OF THE
multitude is to multiply yourself through mentoring.

18:8   PEOPLE AROUND YOU WILL EITHER HOLD YOU
back or help you go forward. Shed your liabilities.
Multiply your assets.

REMEMBER 70 PERCENT OF PERSONNEL
problems are personality conflicts. That is why
chemistry trumps competency when you hire.

18:9

THE HIGH OF SUCCESSFUL LEADERSHIP IS
addictive and can drive other important dimensions
out of your life. Beware!

18:10

TREAT EVERY MEETING LIKE YOU'RE
entering to take a final exam so you will meet
everyone's expectations of excellence.

18:11

NEVER LET YOUR CIRCUMSTANCES
circumvent your calling as a leader.

18:12

Chapter 18

18:13   EVERY DECISION HAS A DOWNSIDE. IF YOU want to multiply your chances for success, minimize the potential for a negative outcome.

18:14   AUTHENTICITY IS THE KEYSTONE OF integrity. Seek to strip all facades from your life.

18:15   LITTLE PROBLEMS OVER TIME CAN PRODUCE the greatest pressures on your life. Take time to solve them.

18:16   A LEADER LEARNS TO SPEAK UP WHEN something is about to go down. When you see it, say something about it.

TRAIN YOURSELF TO REFRAIN FROM
meddling in matters that are not your responsibility.

18:17

PAST PERFORMANCE IS THE GREATEST
indicator of future possibilities and probabilities.

18:18

LEADERSHIP IS AN ADVENTURE TRIP FULL OF
risk and reward. Enjoy it!

18:19

IT'S AMAZING HOW YOU CAN CHANGE THE
behavior of the people on your team just by believing
in them.

18:20

Chapter 18

18:21   IT IS COSTLY TO WASTE A LEADERSHIP mistake by not learning from it the first time you make it.

18:22   LEADERS SET THE TONE IN TIMES OF trouble. Your followers will reflect your reactions and make the situation either better or worse.

18:23   DON'T PROLONG THE IMPACT OF A WRONG decision. Either reverse it or replace it with the right one.

18:24   SERVANT LEADERS WANT THEIR FOLLOWERS to see and know they are genuinely cared about as persons. No one wants to be treated as units of production.

NEVER LET DISAPPOINTMENT OR DESPAIR 18:25
impair your leadership judgment.

THE HARD GRIND BEGINS WHEN YOU START TO 18:26
implement your strategy. Press on and keep things
in perspective. Monitor your progress and your
setbacks.

DEVELOP THE SKILLS TO HELP PEOPLE 18:27
persevere through periods of stress and distress.

DON'T LIVE YOUR PRIVATE LIFE SUCH THAT IF 18:28
it were revealed it would be a public disgrace.

Chapter 18

18:29   KEEP A POSITIVE ATTITUDE REGARDLESS OF what the naysayers are proclaiming. Keep believing! All things are possible to those who believe.

Chapter 19

NEVER ASSUME A LEADER IS effectively leading the charge simply because they are in charge.

19:1

TURN YOUR MESS INTO YOUR MISSION. START a crusade to erase the crisis you face.

19:2

LEADERSHIP DRAINS YOU. PERIODICALLY pause in pursuing your cause to refill your passion bucket.

19:3

PROGRESS AND PROBLEMS ARE INCREASING exponentially. Leaders are needed now more than ever.

19:4

Chapter 19

19:5   IF YOU ARE FIRED UP, DON'T FIRE BACK AND pour gasoline on the flames. Cool off before you comment or someone is going to get hurt.

19:6   LONG MEETINGS ARE INEFFICIENT, frustrating and non-productive. Set a time limit and stick to it. Start and quit on time. Pick up where you left off at the next meeting.

19:7   YOU CAN HAVE A DISSENTING THOUGHT without having a dissenting spirit.

19:8   AS A LEADER, DON'T BE OBLIVIOUS TO THE obvious. Common sense is not that common anymore. Pursuing it gives you a distinct advantage.

THE BEST WAY TO ENGAGE YOUR AUDIENCE IS
to energize your presentation.

19:9

BE FAITHFUL WITH A FEW RESPONSIBILITIES
and your leadership capital will accrue.

19:10

BE METICULOUS IN YOUR PLANNING,
implementing and evaluating. The irresponsible
rarely reach their goals.

19:11

DISCOVER A COMPELLING VISION, DEVELOP A
comprehensive strategy and then relentlessly
implement it.

19:12

Chapter 19

19:13   DEMAND FACTS AND DATA TO SUPPORT EVERY opinion. That triangle is the strongest structure on which to rest your decision.

19:14   BE FLEXIBLE IN YOUR IMPLEMENTATION BUT inflexible in your convictions.

19:15   GREAT LEADERS DON'T LET FRUSTRATIONS derail them from the track to success.

19:16   ALWAYS PROTECT AND INSPECT YOUR objectivity.

STOP MAKING EXCUSES FOR YOUR LACK OF 19:17
execution. Design, assign, time and monitor the tasks
needing to be done.

LEADERS MUST REALIZE EVERYONE IS 19:18
pulling for them. They are either trying to pull them
down or pull them up.

IT IS THE JOB OF LEADERSHIP TO ESTABLISH 19:19
clear parameters and then evaluate performance.

BEING A NICE LEADER CAN BECOME A VICE IF 19:20
you are unwilling to deal with unpleasant problems
and people.

Chapter 19

19:21   ALWAYS CONFRONT CONFLICT BEFORE IT HAS an opportunity to afflict trouble onto your organization.

19:22   DON'T LET YOUR MOTIVATION FOR LEADING become applause and approval. Leadership isn't about you, but rather about taking people from where they are to where they need to go.

19:23   SERVANT LEADERS CARE MORE ABOUT OTHERS than themselves.

19:24   STRONG LEADERS HAVE BEEN STRETCHED AND perfected over time.

WHEN IT COMES TO PROBLEMS, IGNORE THE petty and tackle the weighty.

19:25

HISTORY CAN GUIDE, BUT IT DOES NOT always guarantee.

A SERVANT LEADER ROUTINELY PERFORMS unexpected acts of kindness.

19:26

HISTORY CAN GUIDE, BUT IT DOES NOT always guarantee.

19:27

SERVANT LEADERS ARE MORE CONCERNED about people than projects. The only things that will outlast you are the people you invest in.

19:28

Chapter 19

19:29   THINGS HAVE A TENDENCY TO DERAIL WHEN there is a lack of attention to detail.

19:30   IN LEADERSHIP, YOU ARE REWARDED IN direct proportion to the service you render.

Chapter 20

THE MORE PEOPLE WHO HAVE BOUGHT into the vision, the more money will be brought into the vision.

20:1 _____

SOMETIMES IT IS EASIER TO LEAD ALONE, BUT you will never be as effective in the long run. Give others the opportunity to journey with you.

20:2 _____

THE SPEED OF THE LEADER HAS THE greatest influence on the team. Find the right speed for everyone's success.

20:3 _____

RESPOND APPROPRIATELY TO AN ATTACK. Don't react. You usually just escalate the conflict if you do.

20:4 _____

Chapter 20

20:5   YOU'RE EITHER LOSING OR GAINING GROUND. It is impossible to maintain the status quo.

20:6   DON'T PUNISH YOUR TEAM MEMBERS BY failing to let them know how they are doing— evaluate and communicate.

20:7   THE PATH OF LEAST RESISTANCE DEAD ENDS at the point of least reward.

20:8   STRONG LEADERS WILL RELENTLESSLY AND purposefully pursue their goal until their vision becomes a reality.

THERE ARE TWO KINDS OF PEOPLE—TAKERS 20:9
and makers!

YOU CAN'T BE OBLIVIOUS TO THE OBVIOUS 20:10
and still be successful.

CONSTRAIN YOURSELF FROM CONTRADICTING 20:11
yourself. Consistency is an essential characteristic of
good communication.

THE SERVANT LEADER DOESN'T ACCUMULATE 20:12
power but shares it.

Chapter 20

20:13   WHEN LEADING A GROUP, DON'T BE SCARED
by silence. It can be uncomfortable, but it will be
unprofitable if you squelch it.

20:14   DON'T BE CORNERED INTO A COMPLIMENT.
People can read right through meaningless flattery.

20:15   MAINTAIN THE CONVICTIONS GOVERNING
your leadership regardless of the conditions.

20:16   SERVANT LEADERS PUT THE NEEDS OF OTHERS
before their own. They want each team member to
reach their full potential.

TAKE TIME TO REMEDIATE TEAM MEMBERS
who have time management problems. They either
have a distraction or discipline problem.

20:17

IF YOU DON'T SPEAK AND ACT IN GOOD FAITH,
others will be unfaithful to you.

20:18

AVOID A BREAKDOWN BY BREAKING AWAY
with your team from time to time.

20:19

THERE ARE THREE TYPES OF LEADERS: THOSE
who people love and praise, those who people fear
and flee and those who people hate and undermine.

20:20

Chapter 20

20:21   FAITHFULNESS IN THE FUNDAMENTALS OF leadership ensures a leader's long-term success. Consistently cling to the basics.

20:22   IF YOU DEVELOP LEADERS WHO ARE WISER, action oriented, balanced and have a greater heart for service than you, you are a truly successful leader.

20:23   DEEPER REFLECTION OF THE CONSEQUENCES of an action can sometimes be the best protection against failure.

20:24   A LEADER MUST DEVOTE AMPLE TIME TO research and development of new products and services to stay on the cutting edge.

REMEMBER THE RULE OF CONTEXTUALIZATION:
just because it worked in one context does not
guarantee it will work in the next.

20:25

DON'T BE AN AUTOCRATIC OR LAISSEZ-FAIRE
leader. The first is a hated dictator and the second is
an oxymoron.

20:26

MOTIVATE, TRAIN AND ENABLE YOUR TEAM
members to unfold their full potential in using their
skills and abilities.

20:27

SERVANT LEADERS HAVE A PARTICIPATORY
style that involves team members in decision-making.

20:28

Chapter 20

20:29   THE BEST EXPLANATION IS A GOOD EXAMPLE.

20:30   PARTICIPATORY LEADERSHIP THAT GIVES responsibility and credit results in the highest possible performance and satisfaction by your team members.

Chapter 21

A GUIDED MISSILE CAN'T HIT ITS TARGET without constant reassessment and course corrections. You can't either.

A SERVANT LEADER CONSTANTLY STRIVES TO be trustworthy. Trust is the glue of every great relationship.

21:2

SELF-ASSESSMENT IS CRITICAL FOR SELF-advancement.

21:3

EMPOWER YOUR LEADERSHIP BY EMPOWERING your people.

21:4

Chapter 21

21:5   YOU SERVE YOUR TEAM WELL WHEN YOU HELP
them have commUNITY.

21:6   ACCEPTING THE WORST THAT COULD HAPPEN
averts the waste of worry. Then work to prevent that
outcome.

21:7   A LEADER WITH THE ABILITY TO ANTICIPATE
a problem can better develop a solution before it
becomes a disaster.

21:8   LEADERS DON'T HAVE TO HAVE EVERYTHING
be the best in order to make the best of everything.

WHEN CONFLICTS ARE CONTENTIOUS, SEEK A
mediator. While keeping both sides civil, an objective
perspective can help you find a resolution.

21:9

YOUR WORDS HAVE THE POTENTIAL TO MAKE
things better or worse, so weigh them wisely.

21:10

IT IS HEALTHIER TO COACH THAN TO
control. Sometimes it is helpful to let a team member
make a mistake to learn a lesson.

21:11

IN LEADERSHIP, IT IS NOT SURVIVAL OF THE
fittest; it is survival of the most agile.

21:12

Chapter 21

21:13   DON'T WASTE TIME WORKING WHERE YOU ARE neither welcomed nor wanted.

21:14   THERE IS LITTLE CHANCE OF SUCCESS without a clear plan of leadership succession. Without it, you are likely to have a severe digression in direction.

21:15   AN IGNORANCE OF GOOD GOVERNANCE prevents you from educating your board. You and the entire organization will suffer. Get smart!

21:16   IT'S NOT ALWAYS ADVANTAGEOUS TO BE adventurous. When you assess the risk, it is sometimes just too high.

WHEN IT COMES TO RISK ASSESSMENT, 21:17
calculate carefully.

LEARN TO COLLABORATE WELL SO YOU GIVE 21:18
more than you get. That is the kind of partner
everyone wants.

YOUR MORAL AUTHORITY COMES FROM YOUR 21:19
adherence to absolute truth.

OVER TIME, LEADERS EITHER DEVELOP OR 21:20
destroy the trust of the people on their team. Trust is
the glue keeping an organization from breaking apart.

Chapter 21

21:21   YOU WILL NEVER WIN IF YOU NEVER BEGIN.
Go ahead and get started today.

21:22   VIEW LEADERSHIP AS AN ACT OF SERVICE TO
God and others.

21:23   LEADERS HAVE THE RESPONSIBILITY TO
nurture their own giftedness as well as the gifts of
those who are entrusted to their care.

21:24   SHOW THE PEOPLE YOU WORK WITH THAT YOU
care by carrying out with excellence the
responsibilities that are entrusted to you.

STRAIGHT TALK IS OFTEN REQUIRED TO
straighten out recurring problems.

21:25

YOUR EXEMPLARY RELATIONS WITH YOUR
employees transmutes into their excellent treatment
of your constituency, which leads to high loyalty to
your organization. It all starts with you.

21:26

TRUSTED SERVANT LEADERS ARE ALLOWED TO
bring innovation and change faster. Your team is
willing to risk it because you have their backs.

21:27

YOU WON'T BE ABLE TO LEAD THROUGHOUT
the long haul unless you remain flexible, teachable
and honorable.

21:28

Chapter 21

21:29   YOU CAN ONLY EFFECTIVELY MENTOR A FEW.
Choose wisely for the greatest return on your
investment.

21:30   OTHERS WILL WANT TO PARTNER WITH YOU IF
you give more than you take in time, resources and
credit.

Chapter 22

BE A DELEGATOR, NOT A DICTATOR, WHEN it comes to passing on detailed assignments to the different members on your team.

22:1

SERVANT LEADERS INSPIRE EXTRAORDINARY effort by their team. You won't have to drive them but rein them in so they don't exhaust themselves.

22:2

EFFECTIVE MARKETING IS TYPICALLY THE hallmark of a remarkable company.

22:3

YOU CAN'T KEEP POINTING THE FINGER AND passing the buck to someone else.

22:4

Chapter 22

22:5   GREAT CHALLENGES CATALYZE THE GREATEST passion for change. A severe crisis is the great opportunity for true transformation.

22:6   DON'T LET THE DEAL FALL APART BECAUSE you didn't follow through.

22:7   STRIVE TO NEVER HIDE THE TRUTH. THE consequence for a cover up can be far worse than the actual crime.

22:8   RESPECT, EMPOWER AND ENABLE YOUR TEAM members to exponentially multiply your impact.

IT'S DIFFICULT TO BE A GREAT LEADER 22:9
without a grateful and appreciative spirit.

YOUR HEART FOR SERVANT LEADERSHIP IS SO 22:10
rare that your team will have trouble recognizing it
or believing it will last, while at the same time hoping
it will.

YOU CAN MOVE FROM BAD TIMES TO GOOD 22:11
times with great leadership.

LEADERSHIP IS RISKY LIKE WATER IS WET. 22:12
The two go together. Get used to it.

Chapter 22

22:13 A LEADER CANNOT AFFORD TO INDULGE IN too much WHINE. It can seriously impair your judgment and discernment. When something goes wrong, sober up and get to work finding a solution.

22:14 FEEDBACK IS A GREAT WAY TO HELP SOMEONE move forward. Knowing how you are doing motivates more effort.

22:15 EVALUATE AS A TEAM TO OBTAIN THE advantage of an examination from every vantage point.

22:16 A TRAIN WRECK IS INEVITABLE IF YOU FAIL to continually train every employee. Many organizations derail for failure to give attention to that detail.

OUR FEAR OF OFFENDING PEOPLE CAUSES OUR 22:17
failure to amend the deplorable conditions of our
culture.

LEADERSHIP TODAY IS NOT "PAINT BY 22:18
numbers." You must be creative on the canvas of
circumstances. Practice to perfect your craft.

STRONG LEADERS ARE EASY TO SPOT BECAUSE 22:19
they show:

- Initiative, they don't have to be told what to do
  and take action on their own.

- Innovation, they don't have to do things the way
  they've always been done.

- Inspiration, they know how to inspire and rally
  the team.

- Intuition, they know in their hearts what they
  must do even if they don't know why.

Chapter 22

22:20 INTUITIVE LEADERS DEAL WITH PROBLEMS and possibilities before others recognize them. Intuition is insight without information. If you develop your intuitive skills as a leader, you will have a distinct advantage over the average leader.

22:21 YOUR LEADERSHIP INTUITION IS ENHANCED by experience, as well as by learning from great leaders. Intuition is the product of integrating education and experience throughout your life.

22:22 TO GET THINGS MOVING IN THE RIGHT direction, find the roadblocks impeding your improvement.

22:23 QUIT COMPLAINING. NO ONE WANTS TO follow a whiner.

LEADERSHIP IS ALWAYS MORE EFFECTIVELY
taught through example rather than through
expectations. Followers grasp a clearer vision through
a role model than through standards of conduct
stipulated by a leader.

22:24

SERVANT LEADERS DON'T SELF-SERVE BUT DO
employ self-reflection to facilitate self-improvement.

22:25

DISAPPOINTMENT CAN BE A HUGE
distraction in execution of an idea or a new pursuit.
Don't let a rejection routinely redefine your direction.

22:26

IN ORDER TO MOVE FORWARD TOWARD THE
future, you sometimes have to seek forgiveness for
the past.

22:27

Chapter 22

22:28   CREATE A CUSTOMER CARE POLICY BASED ON accomplishing your goal of great service rather than issuing a list of procedures. This lets your staff customize their actions to fulfill each customer's expectations.

22:29   A STANDARD SET TOO HIGH CAN PUT A strain on the health of those working in your organization. Don't dishearten your greatest asset: your staff.

22:30   STAY ALERT SO YOU ARE QUICK ENOUGH TO swerve when life throws you a curve.

22:31   A PREVIOUS TITLE DOES NOT AUTOMATICALLY entitle you to lead in a different context or culture.

Chapter 23

NEVER LET A LACK OF RECOGNITION BE a restriction on remaining faithful to move forward in what you know you should do. Leading with a servant's heart means it's not about you.

23:1 _____

RELYING ON INFORMATION OBTAINED OUT OF context is dangerous. Take time to understand the situation.

23:2 _____

YOUR PURPOSE IS TO INSTILL A "PURPOSE beyond themselves" into your people.

23:3 _____

CONSISTENCY IS AN IMPORTANT COMPETENCY in leadership. Be careful not to waver in your communication or behavior.

23:4 _____

Chapter 23

23:5   DON'T REFUSE TO IMPROVE AND REUSE AN
old idea. Sometimes the recycled becomes the latest
"new" innovation.

23:6   YOU WOULD BE WISE TO REFRAIN FROM
saying some of the things that pop into your brain.
Ask yourself, "Is this kind, helpful and needed?"

23:7   COMMUNICATE WHAT YOU WANT UP FRONT
and there will be no disappointment, confusion or
surprise.

23:8   YOU CANNOT AFFORD TO HOARD ANY ROOT OF
bitterness. It will eat you from the inside out. With
God's help, expel it and you will heal.

IT IS YOUR LEADERSHIP RESPONSIBILITY TO 23:9
prevent what is bad, preserve what is good and
pursue what is best.

HAVING AN APTITUDE OR ABILITY CAN STILL 23:10
be a limiting factor in leadership without an
accompanying great attitude. Endeavor to possess
both to experience leadership excellence.

THERE IS MORE POTENTIAL ON YOUR TEAM 23:11
than you appreciate. Find and fertilize it so each
person flourishes.

RESIST THE URGE TO STAY ON WHEN IT'S TIME 23:12
to resign. A leader knows in their heart when it's time
to go. No matter the situation, leave with integrity.

Chapter 23

23:13 DON'T LET LIMITED RESOURCES LIMIT YOUR ability to be resourceful. Servant leaders can accomplish a lot with little because they are willing to learn, work harder and take risks.

23:14 INVESTING TO IMPROVE YOUR PEOPLE improves their performance.

23:15 LET YOUR COURAGE BE AN ENCOURAGEMENT to the people around you. They won't accompany the discouraged but will follow the daring.

23:16 A GREAT LEADER HAS LEARNED TO READ their environment. They must read people, problems, possibilities and pitfalls as they scan their surroundings.

A MUNDANE SPIRIT IS A MANDATE FOR change. Fill up your passion reservoir with a new challenge. You can't lead well if you are bored.

23:17

IF YOU HAVE APPLIED YOUR BEST EFFORT TO people who are filled with apathy, it's time to move them on. You cannot make people take ownership and responsibility.

23:18

YOU CAN BE APPOINTED AS A LEADER, BUT people will not follow you if they don't admire you.

23:19

MOST PEOPLE WASTE MOST OF THEIR potential. They fritter away their time on the mundane. You have to stretch to grow.

23:20

Chapter 23

23:21   EVERYONE PERFORMS BETTER WHEN THEY are accountable. What you measure gets done—and done better.

23:22   SERVANT LEADERS DESIRE TO BE HELD accountable. Unmonitored leaders are a danger to themselves and others.

23:23   A LITTLE EVENT CAN HAVE A BIG EFFECT. Something that appears to be insignificant can have an immeasurable long-term impact. Don't despise the little things.

23:24   IF YOU WANT TO BE SELF-FULFILLED, DON'T be selfish.

As David and Mary demonstrate, when God anoints a leader, it has more to do with their SPIRITUAL maturity than with their AGE.

23:25

Loyalty is an elastic ball. When you give it away, it bounces back to you.

23:26

True greatness is not determined by a single moment, but by continual efforts in the right direction.

23:27

It's always good to verify something is true before you pass a story on. Confirm it before you communicate it.

23:28

Chapter 23

23:29   ONE OF THE MARKS OF IMMATURITY IS BEING
more prone to burn a bridge rather than to build one.

Chapter 24

IT'S NOT A GOOD EXAMPLE FOR A LEADER to set expectations for others and then make excuses and exceptions for themselves.

24:1

DON'T HIRE PRIDEFUL PEOPLE.

24:2

SERVANT LEADERS ARE SELF-AWARE, SELF-managed and selfless.

24:3

WORK AS HARD TO BUILD COMMUNITY AMONG your staff as to build your organization. It will increase productivity, decrease staff turnover and make all that time you spend together much more fun.

24:4

Chapter 24

24:5   ALL WORK AND NO PLAY IS DRUDGERY. INFUSE some fun into your workplace.

※

24:6   YOU CAN HAVE A GREATER EFFECT ON someone when you elect to connect with them. Have a genuine interest in finding points of mutual interest.

※

24:7   IF PEOPLE ARE GOING TO BE EFFECTIVELY led, the leader must always be one step ahead of the team.

※

24:8   IT'S WRONG FOR LEADERS TO THINK THEY always have to be right.

SOMETIMES THE HARDEST ITEMS YOU TACKLE   24:9
as a leader will be the most helpful in the long haul.
Don't keep putting them off. Start working on one
today.

A HIGH LEADERSHIP IQ IS NOT HOW MUCH   24:10
you know but how fast and willing you are to learn.

YOU CAN'T TEACH SELF-INITIATIVE. YOU HAVE   24:11
to hire for it. But if you are not careful, you can
regulate it to death.

THE GREATEST OPPORTUNITIES ARE OFTEN   24:12
immediately followed by the greatest obstacles and
opposition.

Chapter 24

24:13   DEMONSTRATE QUALITY, DEMAND QUALITY and determine quality. It is what you must be known for.

24:14   SERVANT LEADERS PRIORITIZE EACH TEAM member's needs, not their feelings. They still need to make unpopular decisions and give negative feedback.

24:15   AN APPEAL TO ACTION IS MUCH MORE attractive than a demand to action. Effective leaders pull people rather than pushing them.

24:16   BE INTENTIONAL AS A LEADER IN RECRUITING and developing interns because there is great reward in the long term.

A LARGE PORTION OF THE MENTORING
process is modeling belief and behavior. Sometimes
the most significant lesson is not in the syllabus or
lesson plan.

24:17

WHEN IT COMES TO MENTORING A LEADER,
the material you use can be immaterial. It's more
about transferring insight than information. Good
material may be helpful, but it does not guarantee the
pupil will graduate to the next level.

24:18

THE MENTORING PROCESS INVOLVES:

24:19

- An intentional element.

- An intellectual element.

- An illustrative element.

- An intangible element.

Chapter 24

24:20 THERE ARE THREE KEY STAGES IN THE
successful mentoring process (1 Timothy 3:9-10):

- Train

- Test

- Trust

24:21 WISDOM IS MORE THAN THE ACCUMULATION
of information. It is the capability of making good
decisions and judgments based on that knowledge
and your experiences.

24:22 WHEN YOU LET SOMEONE PAY FOR THEIR
mistake, they make a wiser decision the next time
they face the same problem.

EVERY PERSON HAS THE POTENTIAL TO BE A leader. Find out how to catalyze its realization.

24:23

YOU WILL NEVER REACH THE CLIMAX OF YOUR leadership potential unless you remain teachable in all things and from all people.

24:24

YOU ONLY HAVE SO MUCH ATTENTION TO give. Focus on two or three things only you can do that will make the greatest difference.

24:25

A LEADER ONLY HAS SO MANY TROOPS. Motivate, train, equip and then deploy them wisely to fight the fewest battles necessary to win the war.

24:26

Chapter 24

24:27   SERVANT LEADERS KNOW EACH OF THEIR colleagues has an intrinsic value beyond their concrete contributions to accomplishing the mission.

24:28   ALL LEADERS MUST BE TESTED BEFORE THEY take a turn leading. As a mentor, make sure you invest in them before you test them.

24:29   WHEN YOU TAKE THE TIME TO PROPERLY prepare, you will spend less time repairing what went wrong.

24:30   DON'T BE AFRAID TO STEP ASIDE FROM TIME to time and let your mentee struggle a little. Struggles stretch and strengthen the student.

Chapter 25

SUCCESS MUST BE MEASURED IF IT IS going to bring pleasure. You can't celebrate unless there is a finish line.

25:1

LEADERS WHO WAFFLE BACK AND FORTH IN their convictions are awful to follow.

25:2

KNOW THE EARLY INDICATORS THAT forecast you are on the pathway to success. That will save time and energy.

25:3

TOO MANY LEADERS ARE MISLED TO BELIEVE luck is what makes people successful. The fact is that most successful leaders just stuck it out longer than everyone else.

25:4

Chapter 25

25:5   YOUR TEAM WANTS TO KNOW IF THEY ARE winning or not as they pursue their goals. Make sure their scorecard is simple and visible at all times.

25:6   YOUR "LAST" PRIORITIES WILL MAKE A lasting impression on those around you and will outlast your leadership. Make a point to prioritize things in your life that will outlive you.

25:7   REGULARLY TAKE SHORT BREAKS TO EXAMINE the score. If you are losing, do some coaching and then ask your team members what they are personally committed to doing so the team will win.

25:8   WHEN YOU'RE WILLING TO TOLERATE anything, you will have to put up with everything.

THREE COMMON PLACEMENT PROBLEMS   25:9
occur when you put people into positions requiring
servant leadership:

- ⤙ Placing people who are NOT leaders into
  positions of leadership.

- ⤙ Placing people who are NOT servants into
  positions of service.

- ⤙ Placing people who lack passion for what needs to
  be done into positions of leadership and service.

SIMPLIFY! SIMPLIFY BUREAUCRACY TO THE   25:10
absolute minimum amount needed. Your team can't
win their race with a heavy bureaucratic weight
chained to their legs.

A LEADER SHOULD BE SO ACUTELY PRECISE   25:11
and accurate that they could be accused of telling the
truth every time.

Chapter 25

25:12   LEADERSHIP IS MORE FORMATION THAN formula. Most developing leaders are looking for the quick formula for success rather than the long-term formation of leadership experience and skills.

25:13   A STANDARD LEADERSHIP PRACTICE IS TO DO the following:

- When someone asks to meet, ask in advance for the topic of conversation to prepare.

- When someone asks a question on the spot and you don't know the immediate answer, ask if you can get back to them as soon as possible.

- When someone asks a question you have to give an immediate answer to, rely on your intuition and the best information available at that moment.

25:14   RETRAIN YOUR BRAIN TO REFRAIN WHEN YOU want to complain.

TOO MANY LEADERS ARE STUCK BECAUSE
they don't know where to start. They are doing
NOTHING because they don't know what to do
NEXT. Turn the process upside down. Start at where
you want to end up and go backward in the steps
required until you arrive at the first one. Begin there.

25:15

SERVANT LEADERSHIP CAUSES A CHAIN
reaction. It moves others to emulation, who move
others, who then move others until everyone is
transformed.

25:16

INTUITION IS DEVELOPED BY EAGERLY
observing and collecting knowledge from your
surroundings at all times. Then tune your conscious
mind to your subconscious mind as you pay attention
to your feelings, emotions and flashes of inspiration.

25:17

Chapter 25

25:18   IT'S IMPORTANT FOR A LEADER TO STAND behind their team over the long haul without being blind to their shortcomings.

25:19   NEVER LET YOUR ORGANIZATIONAL resources limit your organizational reach and impact. With charisma and inspiration, much can be done with little.

25:20   BE VIGILANT AND DILIGENT TO MAKE THE right choices, but if you err, recognize it, recover quickly and rectify your mistake.

25:21   A VIGOROUS VOLUNTEER PROGRAM exponentially increases your influence and your impact.

ONE BAD DECISION CAN HAVE IMMEASURABLE   25:22
consequences. Consider carefully in order to choose
wisely.

YOUR JOB IS TO ENHANCE THE WORTH OF THE   25:23
people you lead every day. Be a value-adding leader.

CONTINUE TO COMMIT YOUR WAYS TO THE   25:24
Lord and your plans will far exceed your wildest
expectations (Psalm 37:5).

SUCCESS IS A STEEP AND DIFFICULT   25:25
mountain worth climbing. You will need the rope
of resolve and the pitons of persistence to reach the
peak.

Chapter 25

25:26   SELFISHNESS IS THE PATH TO MEANINGLESSNESS.
Selflessness is the only road to true significance.

25:27   THE PATH TO IRRELEVANCE IS PAVED WITH
the best of intentions.

25:28   PEOPLE WILL TRY TO HANG ON TO THE
coattails of your success. Shake them off or they will
slow you down or trip you up.

25:29   YOUR FIRST ORDER OF BUSINESS IS TO TAKE
care of your health. You can't lead well without it.

GOOD POLICIES ARE LIKE GOOD FENCES. THEY   25:30
should only tell people where they can't go.

IT'S YOUR PATIENCE THAT OFTEN PRODUCES   25:31
the most progress in the long run.

Chapter 26

A GREAT IDEA IMPLEMENTED AT THE wrong moment can have a woeful outcome. Bad timing is undermining.

26:1 _____

DON'T JUST GO WITH THE FLOW. BE intentional in your living and your work. Where do you want to be? By when do you want to get there?

26:2 _____

NEVER COMPROMISE YOUR CORE BELIEFS because of something your competition is doing.

26:3 _____

ARTICULATION IS CRITICAL IN THE ART OF communication. If people can't comprehend you, they won't follow you.

26:4 _____

Chapter 26

26:5   FAILURE TO LEARN FROM YOUR EXPERIENCES carries a high price tag. It will cost you dearly in your life and your leadership.

26:6   REMEMBER THAT THE FIRST VERSION IS rarely the final version. It is not called a rough draft for nothing. Perfect your product before you circulate your product.

26:7   MANY PEOPLE WANT THE POSITION, THE prestige and the power of leadership but aren't willing to go through the process of learning leadership.

26:8   DISCIPLINED INVESTING TRANSFORMS INTO financial reward. Tenacious investing in people can transform them into servant leaders.

DON'T BE FORCED TO BURN BRIDGES TO YOUR past. Your resume and relationships will always return to either haunt you or help you.

26:9

YOUR FUTURE OPPORTUNITIES WILL BE determined by how dependable you are in your current role. How far you go in leadership is determined by how faithful you are today.

26:10

TRUE LEADERS MOVE UP THE LADDER OF success because they have earned favor, not because they expected it from others.

26:11

MANY POTENTIAL LEADERS GIVE OUT, GIVE IN or give up early in the game. Leadership demands staying power.

26:12

Chapter 26

26:13   TOO MANY LEADERS WANT THE PRIVILEGE OF leadership without paying the price of leadership. Servant leadership doesn't come cheaply.

26:14   WORK OUT THE KINKS BEFORE EVERYONE thinks your idea stinks. There is no margin for error once your product goes to market.

26:15   YOU WON'T BE ANY BETTER THAN THE PEOPLE you hire around you. They will either enhance your leadership or exhaust it.

26:16   WHEN YOU EXECUTE YOUR VISION, DON'T BE timid. Be daring! Be determined!

KEEP THE PROPER PERSPECTIVE ON OTHER 26:17
people's perceptions. A good decision can generate
disdain, disregard or distinction.

TO BE ACCOUNTABLE, YOU NEED TO BE 26:18
vulnerable and accessible to someone.
Accommodating accountability equals integrity.

IT IS USUALLY APPARENT WHEN YOU'RE BEING 26:19
transparent and when you're not.

ABIDE BY THE RULES AND REGULATIONS AND 26:20
you'll be left with nothing to hide.

Chapter 26

26:21   DELEGATE! IF YOU HAVE TO DO EVERYTHING, you either have a trust problem or you hired the wrong people.

26:22   IT'S A GOOD IDEA TO BRIDLE IDLE TIME. TOO much idleness is indolence.

26:23   MOTIVATION BUILT ON GUILT IS A WEAK foundation. It may work for a moment but will not last long.

26:24   NEVER UNDERESTIMATE THE SPUNK OF AN underdog. They can still sneak up and bite you.

PEOPLE LOVE TO ATTACK THE LEADER OF THE 26:25
pack. Anytime you find yourself ahead, people will be
gunning for your head.

ALL LEADERS GET TIRED IN THEIR PURSUIT 26:26
of their desired dreams. Take time to rest, restore and
renew to refill your passion tank.

FORMULATING A STRONG OPINION BASED ON 26:27
insufficient information is unwise.

TRAIN YOURSELF TO REFRAIN YOURSELF FROM 26:28
chasing after possibilities that do not match your
priorities.

Chapter 26

26:29   No matter what title you have earned, there is always something that can be learned from someone who is working for you.

26:30   Servant leaders observe and listen intently because they value everyone's ideas, feedback and participation.

26:31   Commitment overrides convenience. Contemplate the cost before you communicate a commitment.

26:32   Don't worry about what you can't control. You have enough to contend with without creating unnecessary concerns.

SACRIFICE ALONE WILL NOT SUFFICE ON the road to success. It must be strategic sacrifice.

27:1 _____

A LEADER HAS TO FIND THE BALANCE OF being cautious and audacious. Tipping the scales too far in either direction can be dangerous.

27:2 _____

A LEADER SHOULD ALWAYS EXPLORE A complaint before they ignore a complaint.

27:3 _____

THE BEST LEADERSHIP LESSONS ARE LEARNED in real time. The people you mentor gain better insights when you are intentional and situational.

27:4 _____

Chapter 27

27:5   STREAMLINE YOUR PROCESSES AND procedures wherever you can. Simplify your way to higher productivity.

27:6   SOMETIMES YOU HAVE TO MAKE AN exception to your expectations. There are occasionally situations that merit immunity to a rule.

27:7   BE CAREFUL THAT YOUR RULES AND regulations don't restrain innovation and creativity.

27:8   WHAT ARE YOU WILLING TO LEAVE BEHIND SO you can move forward to grasp a strategic opportunity?

DON'T BE THE CHOKE POINT FOR PROGRESS. 27:9 _____

SURVEY PEOPLE FROM TIME TO TIME IN 27:10 _____
order to surpass your current performance.

CUSTOMIZE YOUR PRODUCTS AND SERVICE TO 27:11 _____
reach your targeted customers.

ALWAYS RESERVE THE RIGHT TO REFUSE A 27:12 _____
regularly approved request. A perfunctory approval is
not always the appropriate answer every time.

Chapter 27

27:13   IT'S VERY IMPORTANT TO VERIFY DETAILS. A double check can save you a lot of trouble in the end.

※

27:14   DON'T GET MAD ABOUT SOMETHING YOU HAD an opportunity to influence in a different direction but ignored. A stitch in time and you won't whine.

※

27:15   IT'S YOUR RESPONSIBILITY TO LEAD WHETHER or not your followers are fans of your decision.

※

27:16   CONTINUALLY PERFECT PERSISTENCE AND patience throughout your leadership life.

A KIND WORD WILL TAKE YOU FARTHER
faster.

27:17

DON'T PROLONG A WRONG ONCE YOU
recognize what is right.

27:18

IT'S NICE, BUT NOT NECESSARY, TO BE LIKED
and loved because of your leadership.

27:19

WISE AND CONFIDENT LEADERS ARE WILLING
to invite critique because they are not threatened by
criticism.

27:20

Chapter 27

27:21   A LEADER'S TEMPERAMENT SETS THE temperature in the workplace.

27:22   SERVANT LEADERS LEAP IN TO DO MENIAL acts of service. Your staff will talk more about those than the great things you accomplish.

27:23   THE MISSION STATEMENT THAT APPEARS ON the wall of your office is worthless if you do not adhere to it in practice.

27:24   IF YOU CAN'T FOLLOW WELL, YOU CAN'T LEAD well. There is always someone further down the leadership trail you should pursue.

LOSE YOUR OBJECTIVITY AND YOU LOSE THE
opportunity to lead effectively.

27:25 _____

BE FLEXIBLE WITH YOUR VISION BUT NEVER
with your values.

27:26 _____

SERVANT LEADERS PARADOXICALLY ARE
looked up to not for what they've done but because
of who they are. Their followers know they care more
about them than just accomplishing their vision.

27:27 _____

LIFE IS NOT ALWAYS FAIR. MOVE FORWARD
anyway.

27:28 _____

Chapter 27

27:29   YOU DON'T NEED TO BE IN THE SPOTLIGHT TO
have valuable insight. If you shine in the supporting
cast, you will end up on center stage.

27:30   TAKE THE TIME TO DEAL WITH AN
individual's discipline deficiencies that can slow your
team. The team can't go far dragging a ball and chain.

27:31   SERVANT LEADERS ARE SELF-AWARE,
situationally sensitive and sharply alert to
obstructions and opportunities. They have an inner
serenity that doesn't seek self but service.

Chapter 28

ONE OF THE KEYS TO SUCCESS IS TO start doing the right things consistently and continuously.

28:1

IT'S HARD TO EXPECT OTHERS TO REGULARLY do what you rarely do. Lead by example.

28:2

IF YOU LACK ACCOUNTABILITY IN leadership, it will not be long until you lack credibility.

28:3

PERSUASION IS MORE POWERFUL THAN positional authority. One is likely to garner respect and the other resentment.

28:4

28:5   DON'T GET SO FOCUSED ON YOUR DAY-TO-DAY duties that you don't dream of what the future ought to be.

28:6   FOSTER FORESIGHT—LEARN FROM THE PAST, understand the present and anticipate the future.

28:7   THERE IS A PRICE TO PAY FOR EVERY privilege. If you don't pay, thinking you are entitled, your privilege and your position will be lost.

28:8   SERVANT LEADERSHIP IS FIRST AND foremost about meeting the needs of others—your colleagues, your company and your constituency.

SUCCESS IS A PROCESS, NOT A PRODUCT. IT IS
fueled by sweat, struggle and stick-to-itiveness.

28:9

YOU ARE A STEWARD OF WHAT YOU LEAD. YOU
hold it in trust for all its stakeholders.

28:10

COMPLEX EXECUTION PLANS DON'T WORK.
Keep it simple and make sure every team member
understands your strategy and the score.

28:11

SERVANT LEADERS KNOW THEIR FOLLOWERS
need community, so they build it.

28:12

Chapter 28

28:13   WHILE PARTIALITY IS TOO OFTEN A REALITY, leaders with integrity don't practice it (Proverbs 28:21).

28:14   FOCUS YOUR ENERGIES ON REPAIRING THE relationship rather than repaying someone who treated you badly. Make peace. Don't start a war.

28:15   IN MOMENTS THAT REQUIRE RESOLVE, BE careful not to sound retreat.

28:16   NEVER ASSUME A CLOSE FRIEND IS NOT capable of fraud. Trust but also verify.

DON'T BE CARELESS WITH YOUR CHARACTER. 28:17
It takes years to build but seconds to bust.

YOU WILL DISCOVER THAT THE DARKEST AND 28:18
most difficult moments are when you often learn your
most important lessons.

LEADERS CANNOT ALWAYS SHARE EVERYTHING 28:19
they know with everyone they know. Some
information must be kept confidential.

IF YOU CAN'T KEEP A CONFIDENCE, SOON NO 28:20
one will confide in you.

Chapter 28

28:21   SERVANT LEADERS BUILD CONSENSUS ON A foundation of trust. Both take work to construct and maintain.

28:22   WISE LEADERS WILL CAREFULLY CONSIDER all of their options, even if they are not congruent with their own opinions.

28:23   WHILE EVERYONE HAS THE CAPACITY TO develop their leadership skills, not everyone will have the tenacity to do it.

28:24   SELFISH LEADERS NEVER LEAVE A LASTING legacy. People are glad to see them go.

LEVERAGE WHO YOU KNOW AND WHAT YOU know from the past to build a better future.

28:25

CHALLENGES OFTEN REQUIRE CHANGE. Change requires bold leadership. Give it.

28:26

DON'T LET YOUR COMPETITION COMPROMISE your convictions. Better to be beaten than have your values broken.

28:27

YOU WILL NEVER ACHIEVE WHAT YOU NEVER attempt.

28:28

Chapter 28

28:29 IF YOU SPEND MORE TIME AND ENERGY problem solving than problem fretting, you will discover solutions to your situation.

28:30 WHEN YOU LACK ACCOUNTABILITY, YOU WILL ultimately forfeit your credibility.

28:31 THE POPULAR DECISION IS NOT ALWAYS THE proper decision. Don't take a poll. Make a courageous decision.

Chapter 29

A LEADER SHOULD NOT HESITATE TO SAY
NO when they KNOW saying YES would be a
bad decision.

29:1

A SERVANT LEADER FOCUSES ON OTHERS'
needs, but in doing the right things, you may still
have to hurt their feelings.

29:2

IN THE RACE OF LIFE, LEADERS KEEP THEIR
eyes on the completion of their goals, not their
competition.

29:3

IT'S IMPORTANT TO BRING OTHER LEADERS
along on your journey. Your greatest legacy will be
mentoring future leaders to become better than you.

29:4

29:5   INVIGORATE YOUR IDEAS BY COLLABORATING with your colleagues. Wise leaders know they are not the only ones with good ideas.

29:6   BEING MORE PROACTIVE AS A LEADER CAN help you become more productive as a leader.

29:7   YOU'RE TOO BUSY WHEN YOU'RE TOO BUSY TO give your key staff regular focused time with you.

29:8   IT IS PROFITABLE TO BE PREDICTABLE. WHEN your people know what you expect, it reduces their level of anxiety.

TEAM MORALE WILL EVENTUALLY ERODE
when team members do not carry their own load.

29:9

∗

NEVER ACCEPT WHAT OTHERS CONSIDER TO
be "reality"—change it.

29:10

∗

KEEPING A PROPER PERSPECTIVE ON YOUR
situation will help you persevere through your
situation.

29:11

∗

SERVANT LEADERS INVEST IN PEOPLE BY
sharing networks, resources and wise counsel. Their
"return" is helping others succeed.

29:12

Chapter 29

29:13   CONSCIOUSLY CRAFT A CULTURE OF
continuous improvement.

29:14   GO THROUGH THE PILE ON YOUR DESK. FILE
it where you can find it, when you need it.

29:15   YOU WILL CONTINUE TO ADD CREDIBILITY TO
your leadership by giving credit to those who deserve
it. Give and it shall be given to you.

29:16   UNMANAGED DISAPPOINTMENT WILL SOON
lead to discouragement which will ultimately damage
your visionary leadership.

IF YOU CONSISTENTLY ENFORCE COMPANY
policy, it will be easier to reinforce proper procedures
and protocols.

29:17

DON'T BE SARCASTIC WITH THAT WHICH IS
sacred.

29:18

EMBRACE THE RACE THAT IS SET BEFORE YOU.
Run with perseverance and endurance to reach your
goal.

29:19

PRACTICING SERVANT LEADERSHIP ENHANCES
job satisfaction and leads to greater productivity from
your team.

29:20

Chapter 29

29:21   GOOD LEADERS ARE TASK-ORIENTED,
relationship-focused and promote participative
leadership.

29:22   THE PROBLEM WITH ALWAYS LOOKING
forward is we often regret the moments we missed by
not living in the present.

29:23   LEADERS MUST CLEARLY SAY WHAT THEY
mean and always mean what they say.

29:24   YOUR TRUE LEADERSHIP WILL BEGIN WHEN
you face a "no-win" situation on both sides and are
able to successfully negotiate a "win-win" settlement.

THE WORK INVOLVED IN LEADERSHIP   29:25
typically far outweighs any perk that comes with your
title of leadership.

SO MUCH OF THE OUTCOME OF SPIRITUAL   29:26
leadership hinges on the amount of time you spend in
prayer and in preparing well.

YOU CANNOT FORCE PEOPLE TO GO FARTHER   29:27
and faster than they are willing to go. A good leader
doesn't drive people but is out front urging them on.

IT'S BETTER TO LEAD BY EXAMPLE THAN JUST   29:28
through expectation.

Chapter 29

29:29   SOMETIMES THE PEOPLE YOU TRUST THE MOST will respond with something that will feel very unjust. The people closest to you have the potential to cause you the greatest disappointment and pain.

29:30   A NEGATIVE ATTITUDE AND OUTLOOK WILL almost always prevent a positive impact and influence.

Chapter 30

EXCELLENCE SHOULD NEVER BE implemented incrementally or gradually.

30:1 _____

LEADERSHIP IS SOMETIMES MORE ABOUT asking the right questions than giving the right answers.

30:2 _____

OFTEN A CORRECTION IS THE BEST WAY TO get moving in the right direction. Make it!

30:3 _____

SERVANT LEADERS ARE NOT AUTOCRATIC OR hierarchical. They know success is best achieved through encouraging teamwork and shared decision-making, creating a caring community and helping others develop.

30:4 _____

Chapter 30

30:5   AS A LEADER, YOU HAVE TO BE CAREFUL NOT to let your compassion become calloused over time. That will hurt others and yourself.

30:6   A LEADER SHOULD BE RESPONSIBLE ENOUGH to respond to requests and other communications in a reasonable time frame.

30:7   PERSONAL DEVELOPMENT IS A DAILY discipline, not an occasional occurrence. Constant change means you are either getting smarter or getting dumber.

30:8   DON'T SEND SUBTLE SIGNALS WHEN A strong, straightforward statement is necessary.

TAKING THE TIME TO PROCESS A PROBLEM
verbally is only valuable if you focus on making
progress in solving your predicament. Talk for talk's
sake in a meeting is a waste.

30:9 ____

RESISTANCE TO CHANGE CAN BE JUST AS
costly as the insistence to change for change's sake.

30:10 ____

THE BEST TIME TO DEBATE AN IDEA OR ISSUE
is in the discussion and inception phase, NOT the
initiation or implementation phase.

30:11 ____

A NEGATIVE RESPONSE DOES NOT ALWAYS
demand a new route. Sometimes you just have to stay
the course to win the race.

30:12 ____

Chapter 30

30:13   PEOPLE OFTEN HAVE TO BE INSPIRED TO BE positive, because change is often scary and uncomfortable.

30:14   A LEADER SHOULD NOT THREATEN TO QUIT TO get their way. Protesting like that rarely ends up producing anything positive except an unexpected opportunity to float your resume.

30:15   EXERCISE YOUR LEADERSHIP DAILY TO strengthen your endurance for the unknown challenges ahead.

30:16   TRULY GREAT LEADERS ARE SEEN AS GREAT servants by those who know them best. They can fool the public but not those who know them well.

WHEN IT COMES TO CHANGE, PEOPLE REACT more positively to an evolution rather than a revolution.

30:17

LEADERS OFTEN HAVE TO SIT ON THEIR IDEAS to allow them to mature before they implement those changes.

30:18

THE TOP THREE PRIORITIES OF SERVANT leaders are serving their employees, their customers and their community, knowing their mission will be accomplished if they do those things well.

30:19

YOUNG LEADERS MUST BE PROGRESSIVELY tested before they can be trusted. If they are faithful with a little, they can be given something larger to lead.

30:20

Chapter 30

30:21   INSIST YOUR BOARD HAVE EXECUTIVE SESSION to discuss your performance together at every meeting. Without that opportunity, they will talk about you in unhealthy small factions outside the boardroom.

30:22   A LEADER MUST BE CAREFUL THEIR PERSONAL interactions do not become performance distractions. Your private life has public ramifications.

30:23   APPEALING IS MORE APPROPRIATE THAN commanding and demanding in a demeaning way. You can move forward without being forceful.

30:24   PEOPLE LOVE TO FOLLOW AN AUTHENTIC leader who has passion and purpose.

You will experience appreciation 30:25
depreciation the longer you lead in any given
situation. So make sure appreciation is not the fuel
that fires your engine.

Don't focus so much on what is 30:26
happening next that you neglect what is happening
now. Keep your vision bifocal.

Brief meetings that are planned, 30:27
participatory and to the point are popular.

Electronic reminders are a great way to 30:28
remain on track and on task.

Chapter 30

30:29   MAKE YOUR PROMISE YOUR PRIORITY. MAKE sure you get done what you said you would do on time before tackling something else.

30:30   OVERCOME YOUR ADDICTION OR FACE A leadership eviction. Confess and find an accountability partner.

Chapter 31

IF EVERYONE WHO SUPERVISES ANYONE IS A servant leader, you will markedly reduce the level of stress and strife in your organization. Reducing friction moves you faster to reaching your goals.

31:1

KEEP IN MIND THAT IT IS NOT ALWAYS WISE or appropriate to address a problem with complete candor.

31:2

A LEADER HAS TO KNOW WHEN IT'S appropriate to charge, retreat and retread to start over.

31:3

A GOOD RESUME CAN STILL BE A BAD FIT FOR your organization if the person doesn't have good character and good chemistry with your team.

31:4

Chapter 31

31:5   A PRESSURE COOKER WILL BLOW UP IF something blocks its vent. An organization will blow up if you let someone constantly obstruct its progress. In both situations, promptly remove the impediment to avoid an explosion.

31:6   ARROGANCE IN LEADERSHIP LEADS TO turbulence in the workplace.

31:7   ONE OF THE BEST WAYS TO SHAPE YOUR future success is to sharpen your current skills. Be intentional in your investment in your personal growth.

31:8   EVERY ORGANIZATION HAS ITS OWN SPEED limit for driving change. Make sure you notice the local road signs so you don't pay the penalty for going too fast.

SUCCESS CAN CAUSE COMPLACENCY. YOU NEED 31:9
to expand your vision and set new goals or your
organization will slow down, drop into a rut and spin
its wheels.

IF YOU WANT TO HIRE EMPLOYEES WHO 31:10
inspire confidence in your company, you can never
leave that process up to coincidence. The most
important thing a leader must do is to hire the right
people.

TO BE AN EFFECTIVE LEADER, YOU MUST 31:11
understand the gist of logistics and have good sense
in setting up systems.

TO ACCOMPLISH THE IMPOSSIBLE, WORK 31:12
backward from the final goal, step by step, and then
do the first thing.

Chapter 31

31:13   ALL GREAT LEADERS KNOW THE DIFFERENCE
between being entitled and being entrusted.

31:14   LEADERS HAVE TO LEARN HOW TO MASTER
the art of "right sizing." It is an opportunity to trim
out the gristle and fat so everything works better.

31:15   DON'T SWEAT IT! REMEMBER, OPPOSITION
provides an opportunity for real leadership.

31:16   COMMON SENSE IS THE SHADOW OF TRUTH.
That is why without absolute truth, everything gets
ridiculous real fast.

YOU ARE RESPONSIBLE FOR YOUR
organization. Seek wise council, then take the heat
and don't retreat from your convictions.

31:17

MORE ORGANIZATIONS FAIL DUE TO POOR
governance than poor leadership. Invest time in
training your board.

31:18

IF YOU LOSE THE CONFIDENCE OF YOUR
board or your stakeholders, gracefully bow out
before it gets nasty.

31:19

CHART YOUR COURSE BEFORE YOU START
your course (Luke 14:28-32). You can't reach your
goal unless you know what it is.

31:20

Chapter 31

31:21   AVOIDING CRITICISM AT ALL COST CAN become extremely costly.

31:22   YOU CAN HANDLE ANYTHING WITHIN REASON for a season. Endurance and resilience are strengths of great leaders.

31:23   ELIMINATE AN ELITE MENTALITY IN YOUR organization. Throw conceit out on the street. It is not about "me" but about "we."

31:24   A SERVANT LEADER IS THE "FIRST AMONG equals." They lead but don't see themselves more important than anyone else. They serve others, not themselves.

THE PACKAGING IS JUST AS IMPORTANT AS
the product. Wrap it well and it will sell.

31:25

BELIEVE IN YOUR PEOPLE AND THEY WILL
become more than they ever dreamed.

31:26

DON'T ALLOW YOUR LEADERSHIP AMBITIONS
to ambush God's purpose for your life. You won't get
ahead in life if you get ahead of God.

31:27

NEVER MAKE A RADICAL DECISION WITHOUT
considering the potential radical consequences of that
decision.

31:28

Chapter 31

31:29   LET YOUR SUCCESS BE CREDITED TO OTHERS, not at the expense of others.

31:30   SERVANT LEADERS TRY TO BUILD CONSENSUS but still have to make the decisions. They go out of their way to let their team know "why."

31:31   SUBMITTING TO THE LORDSHIP OF CHRIST will transform your leadership.

Appendix A

THE 7 FUNDAMENTALS OF LEADERSHIP

Being faithful to fundamentals is instrumental to long-term leadership success.

1. CHARACTER AND INTEGRITY

Knowing who you are and an unbending commitment to excellent values.

2. TRUST AND CONFIDENCE

Having an ability to inspire faith in others that you will do the right things.

3. VISION AND DREAMS

Knowing where you are headed.

4. INTUITION AND STRATEGY

Knowing how to get to where you want to be.

5. DETERMINATION AND HARD WORK

Willing to have an unrelenting expenditure of your energy.

6. TEAMWORK AND NETWORKS

Realizing you can't get there alone but must value and utilize others to accomplish your vision.

7. OBSERVATION AND EVALUATION

Having situational awareness.

Appendix B

PROBLEM POLICY

1. DON'T POINT OUT PROBLEMS WITHOUT SHARING SOME positive elements as well, if possible. You will negate your influence if you are continuously negative.

2. DON'T POINT OUT PUNY PROBLEMS THAT ARE insignificant.

3. DON'T POINT OUT A PROBLEM UNLESS YOU ARE prepared to point out a possible solution.

4. DON'T WASTE YOUR TIME COMPLAINING ABOUT A problem when you are unwilling to change your course of action.

5. DON'T GO PUBLIC WITH A PROBLEM UNTIL YOU HAVE communicated privately with the person who has caused the problem.

6. DON'T ENGAGE SOMEONE ELSE WITH A PROBLEM WHILE making excuses for yourself regarding the same issue. (That's called hypocrisy. Yank the plank from your own eye first.)

7. DON'T MAKE ANOTHER PROBLEM WHILE ATTEMPTING TO fix your problem.

8. DON'T LISTEN TO A COMPLAINT FROM SOMEONE WHO has not already confronted the person directly involved or responsible.

9. DON'T TAKE SIDES REGARDING A PROBLEM UNLESS YOU have witnessed it firsthand or gathered enough secondhand information from both sides of the situation.

10. **DON'T WAIT TO POINT OUT INFORMATION ABOUT A** problem until it's too late. Leaders learn to anticipate potential problems in advance. Whenever possible, resolve potential problems before they evolve. Leaders learn to gauge "problem probability."

11. **DON'T TRY TO RESOLVE A PROBLEM BEFORE YOU** research and understand all of the dynamics of the problem. There may be a good reason why the situation is being handled that way.

12. **DON'T DEAL WITH A PROBLEM WITHOUT CONSULTING** someone in authority within your organization.

13. **DON'T THINK YOU CAN SOLVE A HUGE PROBLEM** without gathering the smartest and wisest people you know to think it through thoroughly.

14. **DON'T BUY INTO THINKING A TOUGH PROBLEM CAN BE** completely solved with an easy decision. Most decisions (especially to difficult problems) don't come with an easy button. In fact, to solve the most difficult problems, you sometimes have to make some of the most difficult leadership decisions of your life.

15. **DON'T RELY ON A POLICY TO PREVENT YOUR PROBLEMS.** While policies and procedures are essential to organizational health, they will not eliminate all of your problems.

Appendix C

LEADERSHIP MYTH BUSTERS

A leadership myth is something we have been taught, trained or told that does not hold up under the examination of experience.

MYTH   A great title is vital to be able to lead.

TRUTH   A title is not a necessity for a true leader.

MYTH   You have to be in charge in order to effectively lead change.

TRUTH   You can effectively influence change from any level.

MYTH   Born leaders make better leaders.

TRUTH   Leadership can be learned.

MYTH   Every person has the potential to be a great leader.

TRUTH   Some people are just NOT designed for leadership.

MYTH   The grass is greener on the other side.

TRUTH   Every setting has its setbacks.

MYTH   Money and moving up the ladder are always the great motivators of leaders.

TRUTH   Lack of adequate compensation is a demotivator, but leaders are motivated by their vision and passions.

MYTH   When things are going well, you can tell there is a good leader at the top.

TRUTH   There is a good leader in charge somewhere in the organization—not necessarily at the top.

MYTH   Bigger is better.

TRUTH   Better is better.

MYTH   If it worked before, it will work again. Likewise, if it worked there, it will work here.

TRUTH   Current success is not always a clear indicator of future success. There are many external factors that differ and will affect the outcome.

MYTH   When you promote people, they will perform better and produce more.

TRUTH   If they are not doing it now, they won't do it then.

MYTH   Visionary leaders don't have to deal with details, just the big picture.

TRUTH   If they don't deal with the details, they won't be leading very long.

MYTH   Great leaders possess charismatic and magnetic personalities.

TRUTH   Some great leaders have little personality at all.

Appendix C

MYTH   The person who holds the highest position is the person leading the organization.

TRUTH   The person with the most influence is leading the group.

MYTH   Education is the best preparation for a leadership position.

TRUTH   More education does not necessarily mean more wisdom. And while education is important, it is experience that makes the ultimate difference.

MYTH   The leader knows it all and has all the answers.

TRUTH   The leader knows who knows. A leader cannot have a complete knowledge of everything. That is why they have to have the right people with the right skills on their team.

MYTH   Leadership gets easier with more experience.

TRUTH   The higher you go in leadership, the harder it gets—no matter how much experience you have.

MYTH   Your personal life has no direct impact on your professional life.

TRUTH   Your personal life and your professional life are intimately intertwined.

MYTH   No one is irreplaceable.

TRUTH   Positions are not irreplaceable—but some people are.

MYTH   Your age can limit your advancements.

TRUTH   Your actions, accomplishments and attitudes will determine your future.

MYTH   The person with the best qualifications gets the job.

TRUTH   The person with the best connections or who makes the best impression gets the job.

MYTH   Leaders have to be loud and demanding to get people's attention.

TRUTH   You don't have to be mean to mean business.

MYTH   It's lonely at the top.

TRUTH   Effective leaders will surround themselves with a great team.

Appendix D

Our Favorite Leadership Lines

"Vision without execution is hallucination." —Unknown

"Some spiritual leaders try to be more committed. What they need is to be more submitted." —Henry T. Blackaby

"A good leader can make up in diligence what they lack in brilliance." —Chuck Swindoll

"Leadership is the art of disappointing people at a rate they can stand." —John Ortberg

"If you find yourself in a hole, stop digging." —Unknown

"Vision is foresight with insight based on hindsight." —George Barna

"Vision is seeing the invisible and making it visible." —George Barna

"The conventional definition of management is getting work done through people, but real management is developing people through work." —Agha Hasan Abedi

"Always practice simplicity with constant repetition, and you will be successful."—John Wooden

"It is the capacity to develop and improve their skills that distinguishes leaders from followers." —Warren Bennis and Burt Nanus

"Beware of spending too much time on matters of too little importance." —Unknown

"Success means doing the best we can with what we have. Success is the doing, not the getting; in the trying, not the triumph. Success is a personal standard, reaching for the highest that is in us, becoming all that we can be." —Zig Ziglar

"No man ever reached excellence in any one art or profession without having passed through the slow and painful process of study and preparation." —Horace

"The best example of leadership is leadership by example." —Jerry McClain

"Be quick—but don't hurry." —John Wooden

"Effective leadership is the willingness to sacrifice for the sake of predetermined objectives." —Ted Engstrom

"Relevance is using what is cultural to say what is timeless." —Reggie Joiner

"The best leaders today are master users of stories, images and symbols." —Tom Peters

"Innovation distinguishes between a leader and a follower." —Steve Jobs

"The ability to summon positive emotions during periods of intense stress lies at the heart of effective leadership." —Jim Loehr

"A leader is one who influences a specific group of people to move in a God-given direction." —J. Robert Clinton

Appendix D

"When it comes to change, there are three seasons of timing: People change when they hurt enough that they have to, when they learn enough that they want to, and when they receive enough that they are able to." —John Maxwell

"Courage is not limited to the battlefield or to the Indianapolis 500 or bravely catching a thief in your house. The real tests of courage are ... the inner tests, like remaining faithful when nobody's looking, like enduring pain when the room is empty, like standing alone when you're misunderstood." —Charles R. Swindoll

"As a leader, you're probably not doing a good job unless your employees can do a good impression of you when you're not around." —Patrick Lencioni

"Bigger is not better—better is better." —Unknown

"The passage of time allows passions to cool, results to clarify, and scholars to compare different approaches." —George W. Bush

"All organizations do change when put under sufficient pressure. This pressure must be either external to the organization or the result of very strong leadership." —Bruce Henderson

"Very often a change of self is needed more than a change of scene." —Arthur Christopher Benson

"Change is inevitable—except from a vending machine." —Robert C. Gallagher

"Make your life a mission—not an intermission." —Arnold Glasgow

Servant Leadership

"To finish first, you must first finish." —Rick Mears

"A competent leader can get efficient service from poor troops, while on the contrary an incapable leader can demoralize the best of troops." —General of the Armies of the United States John J. Pershing

"The leader has to be practical and a realist, yet must talk the language of the visionary and the idealist." —Eric Hoffer

"A dream is just a dream. A goal is a dream with a plan and a deadline." —Harvey Mackay

"If you fail to plan, you plan to fail." —Unknown.

"It's better to look ahead and prepare than to look back and regret." —Jackie Joyner-Kersee

"The essence of strategy is choosing what not to do." —Michael Porter

"The main thing is to keep the main thing the main thing." —Stephen Covey

"A leader's role is to raise people's aspirations for what they can become and to release their energies so they will try to get there." —David R. Gergen

"The person who knows 'how' will always have a job. The person who knows 'why' will always be their boss." —Diane Ravitch

"Leaders conceive and articulate goals that lift people out of their petty preoccupations and unite them in pursuit of objectives worthy of their best efforts." —John Gardner

Appendix D

"Discipline yourself and others won't need to." —John Wooden

"The value of a leader is directly proportional to that leader's values."
—Unknown

"Obstacles are those frightful things you see when you take your eyes
off your goal." —Henry Ford

"If you want your dreams to come true, you mustn't oversleep."
—Unknown

"One thing you can give and still keep...is your word." —Unknown

"Accept that misunderstanding is the occupational hazard of leadership
and stay the course." —Chuck Swindoll

"It has been said that if you want to find gratitude, look in the
dictionary." —Warren Wiersbe

"Leaders who doubt that success is possible and who fear the worst
should immediately change their attitude or resign so a true leader can
take their place." —Henry T. Blackaby

"The ultimate measure of man is not where he stands in moments of
comfort and convenience, but where he stands at times of challenge
and controversy." —Dr. Martin Luther King, Jr.

"Successful leaders see the opportunities in every difficulty rather than
the difficulty in every opportunity." —Reed Markham

"Great leaders are like homemade bread—they rise to the occasion."
—Reed Markham

"Great leaders don't make excuses. They make things better. They are not unrealistic or blind to the difficulties they face. They simply are not discouraged by them. They never lose confidence that the problems can be solved. They maintain a positive attitude. Great leaders don't blame their people for not being where they ought to be; they take their people from where they are to where they need to be. Great leaders never lose faith that this is possible." —Henry T. Blackaby

"When everyone is thinking the same, no one is thinking." —John Wooden

"Not everything that is faced can be changed. But nothing can be changed until it is faced." —James Arthur Baldwin

"Live your life that in such a way that you have nothing to prove, nothing to lose and nothing to hide." —Mark Lowry

"Leaders who experience a lack of discovery may be suffering from a lack of difficulty." —Reed Markham

"Some leaders delegate to deflect responsibility. Other leaders delegate to develop people." —Justin Reinig

"Show me a company that is not customer centered and I will show you a company that is failing to be competitive." —Reed Markham

"Wherever you are, be all there! Live to the hilt every situation you believe to be the will of God." —Jim Elliot

"'I must do something' will always solve more problems than 'Something must be done.'" —Unknown

Appendix D

"A good follow-through is just as important in management as it is in bowling, tennis, or golf. Follow-through is the bridge between good planning and good results." —Anonymous

"To the world you may be one person, but to one person, you may be the world." —Mark Nolan

"The difference between ordinary and extraordinary is just that little extra." —Unknown

"You will never fulfill your destiny doing work that you despise." —John Maxwell

"It's nice to be important, but it's more important to be nice." —Unknown

"Vision without action is a daydream. Action without vision is a nightmare." —Japanese Proverb

"Excellence is taking every assignment seriously for the glory of God." —Kent Crockett

"Plan your work. Then work your plan." —Unknown

"Remember: First class leaders hire first class staff; second class leaders hire third class staff!" —Unknown

"Planning without action is futile, action without planning is fatal." —Unknown

"I am a man of fixed and unbending principles, the first of which is to be flexible at all times." —Everett Dirksen

"What chance gathers she easily scatters. A great person attracts great people and knows how to hold them together." —Johann Wolfgang Von Goethe

"Our greatest fear should not be of failure but of succeeding at things in life that don't really matter." —Francis Chan

"A big man is one who makes us feel bigger when we are with him." —John Maxwell

"Creativity is just connecting things. When you ask creative people how they did something, they feel a little guilty because they didn't really do it; they just saw something. It seemed obvious to them after a while. That's because they were able to connect experiences they've had and synthesize new things." —Steve Jobs

"Blessed is he who has learned to admire but not envy, to follow but not imitate, to praise but not flatter, and to lead but not manipulate." —William Arthur Ward

"Sometimes all you need is 20 seconds of insane courage." —*We Bought a Zoo*

"Never confuse prominence with significance." —Rick Warren

"Integrity doesn't require perfection, but it does require consistent sincerity." —Wess Stafford

"Leaders are dispensable but leadership is indispensable." —Unknown

"Take time out to focus on what you're really all about." —David Long

Appendix D

"Genius is the ability to reduce the complicated to the simple."
—C.W. Ceran

"It is the capacity to develop and improve their skills that distinguishes leaders from followers." —Warren Bennis

"Act your wage." —Dave Ramsey

"If you cannot explain something simply, you don't know enough about it." —Albert Einstein

"What we say is true and forthcoming—not just technically correct."
—Dell Inc.'s Code of Conduct

"There is a choice you make in everything you do. So keep in mind that in the end, the choice you make, makes you." —John Wooden

"What matters most is not the honor that you take with you, but the heritage you leave behind." —Branch Rickey

"Always be a first-rate version of yourself, not a second-rate version of someone else." —Judy Garland

"Be who you are and say what you feel because people who mind don't matter and people who matter don't mind." —Dr. Seuss

"The elevator to success is out of order. You'll have to use the stairs... one step at a time." —Joe Girard

"Men show their character in nothing more clearly than by what they find laughable." —Anonymous

"Character cannot be developed in ease and quiet. Only through my experience of trial and suffering can the soul be strengthened, ambition inspired, and success achieved." —Helen Keller

"If you were going to die soon and had only one phone call you could make, who would you call and what would you say? And why are you waiting?" —Stephen Levine

"Don't give bonus points for baseline behavior." —Vik Serafin

"Without direction, you will easily yield to distractions."
—T. Lisle Whitman, MD

"Comparison is the root of all dissatisfaction." —David Hull

"One of the secrets of life is to make stepping stones out of stumbling blocks." —Jack Penn

"It's only weird if it doesn't work." —Unknown

"Leaders accomplish their visions through personal growth and personnel growth." —John Maxwell

"If all you give are orders, then all you'll get are order-takers."
—Captain D. Michael Abrashoff

"You cannot change your destination overnight, but you can change your direction overnight." —Jim Rohn

"There is a direct connection between finding your passion and reaching your potential." —John Maxwell

Appendix D

"There are two great days in a person's life: the day you were born and the day you discover why." —Unknown

"A Godly leader finds strength by realizing his weakness, finds authority by being under authority, finds direction by laying down his own plans, finds vision by seeing the needs of others, finds credibility by being an example, finds loyalty by expressing compassion, finds honor by being faithful, finds greatness by being a servant."
—Roy Lessin

"What happened yesterday is history. What happens tomorrow is a mystery. What we do today makes a difference—the precious present moment." —Nick Saban

"Tentative leadership kills the spirit of the whole organization. It's better to leave too soon than to stay too long." —Hans Finzel

"The man who keeps busy helping the man below him won't have time to envy the man above him." —Henrietta Mears

"The bad news is time flies. The good news is you're the pilot."
—Michael Altshuler

"Vision is the world's most desperate need. There are no hopeless situations, only people who think hopelessly." —W. Newman

"Discipline and demand without being demeaning." —Don Meyer

"You do not determine a man's greatness by his talent or wealth, as the world does, but rather by what it takes to discourage him."
—Dr. Jerry Falwell

"You are not what you think you are...but what you think—you are."
—Norman Vincent Peale

"Leadership is stewardship. It's temporary and you're accountable."
—Andy Stanley

"Teamwork is what makes common people capable of uncommon results." —Pat Summitt

"Never allow a person to tell you no who doesn't have the power to say yes." —Eleanor Roosevelt

"If you're going to make every game a matter of life or death, you're going to have a lot of problems. For one thing, you'll be dead a lot."
—Dean Smith

"Not everything that counts can be counted, and not everything that can be counted counts." —Sign hanging in Albert Einstein's office at Princeton

"Planning without action is futile, action without planning is fatal."
—Cornelius Fitchner

"Four steps to achievement: Plan purposefully. Prepare prayerfully. Proceed positively. Pursue persistently." —William A. Ward

"The Lord doesn't ask about your ability, only your availability; and, if you prove your dependability, the Lord will increase your capability."
—Unknown

"Honor is better than honors." —Abraham Lincoln

Appendix D

"The person who does things that count, doesn't usually stop to count them." —Albert Einstein

"Of your unspoken words, you are the master; of your spoken words, the servant; of your written words, the slave." —Quaker Proverb

"The price for lack of focus is elimination." —John Pettus

"Where there is vision there is provision." —Unknown

"It's not what you achieve, it's what you overcome. That's what defines your career." —Carlton Fisk

"The difference between interest and passion is action." —Tim Elmore

"Focus on giants—you stumble. Focus on God—giants tumble." —Max Lucado

Servant Leadership

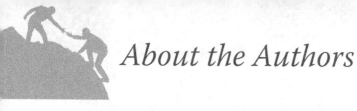

About the Authors

DAVID STEVENS, M.D., M.A. (ETHICS)
CHIEF EXECUTIVE OFFICER EMERITUS

Dr. David Stevens served as the Chief Executive Officer of the Christian Medical & Dental Associations, the nation's largest faith-based organization of doctors for 25 years. Dr. Stevens, as spokesman for 19,000 Christian healthcare professionals, has conducted over 2000 media interviews on bioethical, public policy and scientific issues, including CBS Evening News, ABC World News, MSNBC, BBC-World Television, CNN Sunday Morning, Newsweek, FOX News, PAX-Television, Tech TV, Associated Press, *JAMA*, *USA Today*, Family News in Focus, National Public Radio and many other national outlets.

Prior to his service with CMDA, Dr. Stevens served as medical director of World Medical Mission. In Somalia, Dr. Stevens led an emergency medical team that treated 45,000 suffering Somalis in the midst of war. In the Sudan, medical teams under his leadership treated over 25,000 villagers to stop the spread of an epidemic.

From 1981 to 1991, Dr. Stevens was a missionary doctor at Tenwek Hospital in Bomet, Kenya where he served as Medical Superintendent and Executive Officer. At Tenwek, he directed a $4 million development plan, secured the installation of an $850,000 hydroelectric plant, oversaw the start of a nursing school, and doubled the size of the hospital. The community health care and development programs he designed at Tenwek are currently reaching over a million Kenyans and serves as an example of what medical outreach in the developing world can accomplish.

Dr. Stevens' experiences provide rich illustrations for inspirational and educational presentations at seminars, medical schools, conferences, and churches. His topics include stem cell research, human cloning, genetics, faith and health, physician assisted suicide, international and community-based health care, emergency medical relief, abortion, and other medically related subjects. He is the author of *Jesus, MD, Beyond Medicine* and co-author of *Leadership Proverbs* and *Servant Leadership* and writes many chapters and magazine articles. He is in demand to preach in local churches and at mission conferences.

Dr. Stevens holds degrees from Asbury University, is an AOA graduate of the University of Louisville School of Medicine. He earned a master's degree in bioethics from Trinity International University in 2002. Stevens serves on the board of Asbury University, as a Fellow of the Biotechnology Policy Council of the Wilberforce Forum and is on the Advisory Council of the Center for Bioethics and Human Dignity.

He has regularly taught at the Christian Medical & Dental Associations' educational seminars for missionary physicians and dentists in Kenya, Malaysia, and other forums. He was a catalyst for starting the Global Missionary Healthcare Conference, trains new healthcare missionaries three times a year and annually leads a Summit for executives of mission organization which are doing healthcare ministry. He was a founder of the National Embryo Donation Center. Dr. Stevens and his wife, Jody, have a son Jason, and two daughters, Jessica and Stacy and eleven grandchildren.

The Christian Medical & Dental Associations is a national organization of Christian doctors that seeks to *change hearts in healthcare*. Founded in 1931, CMDA promotes positions and addresses policies on health care issues; conducts overseas and domestic healthcare projects; coordinates a network of Christian doctors for fellowship and professional growth; sponsors student organizations in medical and dental schools; distributes educational and inspirational resources; holds marriage and family conferences; provides international doctors with continuing education resources; and conducts academic exchange programs overseas. CMDA was voted as one of the Best Christian Places to Work, a study commissioned by Christianity Today.

Rev. Bert L. Jones

Pastor Bert serves as the Director of Leadership & Church Relations for the Christian Medical & Dental Associations (CMDA) in Bristol, TN. In this role, Bert oversees the Center for Well-being and Church Ministries. Bert also serves as the Chaplain of CMDA.

Since 1988 Bert has led multiple teams across the street and around the world. Bert has traveled on five different Continents and to over 33 different Countries to teach and preach the Gospel. He has engaged in Leadership development nationally and internationally throughout his ministry.

Bert holds his ordination through the Missionary Church USA. The Missionary Church is an evangelical denomination committed to Church planting and world missions. Bert is under special appointment from the Missionary Church to CMDA.

Prior to rejoining the staff of CMDA, Bert served as the Senior Pastor of Woodburn Missionary Church (from 2014-2021) and as the President & CEO of GO InterNational. Bert previously served on the CMDA staff as Chaplain and Director of Leadership & Church Ministries. In 1998 Bert planted Harvest Community Church in Kittanning, PA and served as its Lead Pastor. Bert has served both in the local church and in Parachurch organizations throughout his ministry.

Bert has coauthored two books with Dr. David Stevens, published by the CMDA. *Leadership Proverbs* was published in 2010 followed by *Servant Leadership* in 2017. Bert is also the author of *Practical Youth Ministry* published by Bristol Books.

About the Authors

Bert grew up as no stranger to the ministry & evangelism. His father and grandfather were both involved in full-time ministry and evangelism. Bert grew up traveling with his family in music and evangelistic ministries. Bert was active in their family radio ministry that was on the air for over 50 years on more than 50 different radio stations around the country (a ministry that his grandparents started). His grandmother was the author of the Hymn "*In Times Like These.*"

Bert graduated from Asbury University in 1989 with a degree in Bible. Bert completed 2 years of Seminary at Pittsburgh Theological Seminary.

Bert and his wife Cheryl have been married since 1989 and have three children: Joshua, Allyson and Aaron. His wife Cheryl is a teacher and is very active in their ministry.

Bert currently serves on several leadership boards. He serves as the Moderator on the General Oversight Counsel (GOC) and Constitution committee for the Missionary Church USA and Has served on the World Partners advisory board and the board of directors at GO InterNational. He currently serves in an advisory capacity as "Past President" for the ministry of GO InterNational.

For more information about the ministry of Bert Jones and Christian Medical and Dental Associations visit *cmda.org*

Notes

Notes

Notes

Notes